rEvolution

Bill Lucas

D1343993

rEvolution

How to thrive in crazy times

Bill Lucas

Crown House Publishing Limited
www.crownhouse.co.uk
www.crownhousepublishing.com

First published by

Crown House Publishing Ltd
Crown Buildings, Bancyfelin, Carmarthen, Wales, SA33 5ND, UK
www.crownhouse.co.uk

and

Crown House Publishing Company LLC
6 Trowbridge Drive, Suite 5, Bethel, CT 06801-2858, USA
www.crownhousepublishing.com

British Library Cataloguing-in-Publication Data
A catalogue entry for this book is available
from the British Library.

ISBN 978-184590129-5

LCCN 2008936753

Printed and bound in the UK by
The Cromwell Press Group, Trowbridge, Wiltshire

Mixed Sources
Product group from well-managed
forests and other controlled sources
www.fsc.org   Cert no. TT-COC-2082
FSC   © 1996 Forest Stewardship Council

Acknowledgments

Special thanks to:

My friend and colleague Professor Guy Claxton, who gave me invaluable advice on an earlier draft.

Colleagues at the University of Hertfordshire who encouraged me to put some of the theories I have described into practice as part of their change programme, UH Evolution.

Jeffrey Defries, Dr Peter Honey, Lynne Sedgmore, Professor Eugene Sadler-Smith, Ruth Spellman, Professor Bob Fryer and Simon Walker, who kindly reviewed the book.

And to the many people mentioned in the book whose ideas have greatly stimulated my own.

Contents

Introduction   1

Rule 1 – Change is changing
Crazy times   20

Rule 2 – Real change is internal not external
It's all about us   48

Rule 3 – Slow down
Life in the fast lane   66

Rule 4 – We can all change the way we see the world
Pioneers and stay-at-homes   92

Rule 5 – We can all learn how to change more effectively
Adaptive intelligence   116

Rule 6 – No one can make you change
It's a free world   146

Rule 7 – Sometimes it's smart to resist
The algebra of change   166

Rule 8 – Use the brainpower of those around you
Six degrees and a flat world   192

Rule 9 – Make up your own rules
End piece   218

Selected Bibliography   225
Index   231

Introduction

It's not the strongest of the species that survive, nor the most intelligent but the ones most responsive to change.

Charles Darwin

We have reached a turning point in our development as a species.

Our past is catching up with us with respect to climate change. We continue to reduce our stock of biodiversity in ways that we do not understand. The population of the planet is expanding so fast that we may not have enough food or water to go round. Whether through religious extremism or shortage of resources the chance of violence and even war is increasing. So serious is the challenge facing Homo sapiens that eminent Professor Martin Rees, President of the Royal Society in the UK, considers that we have only a fifty-fifty chance of surviving this century.

At the same time we continue to get smarter. In the last decade alone just three inventions illustrate our creativity. We have discovered the three billion DNA letters of our own human code – the human genome, invented a hybrid car that runs on petrol and electricity and, in YouTube, found an almost instant means of sharing moving images across the globe. Technological advances involving the Internet, computers and affordable air travel proceed at an astonishing pace so that pretty much wherever we are on the planet, we can be in touch with each other. We are consequently no longer subject to the old rules of time and place. And as the World Wide Web grows exponentially, we are surrounded by so much data that even an educated person could only ever presume to know a tiny fraction of what there is to know.

A century and a half ago Charles Darwin published his brilliant account of the process of evolution, *On the Origin of Species*. His theory of natural selection focused on the way modifications (changes) in species take place over long periods of time. Although he speculated about human beings and their development, his main interest was in the evolution of non-sentient organisms and on the ways in which improvements are passed down the generations so that the species which are most responsive thrive.

Fast forward to today. Evolution is taking place at such a speed that where natural selection took place over millions of years, it is conceivable that human beings may evolve into something else in a matter of a few centuries or less. The essence of Darwin's theory – his emphasis on adaptability as the best strategy for success – holds good. But it does not go far enough in explaining what we might actually do to stay sane and thrive in a period of accelerated evolution.

Homo sapiens has upset the old order by his capacity to turn ideas into actions so rapidly. For precisely because we can think and use language, our evolution is likely to be charted through the quality of our mindware or, as I will refer to it from time to time, our "adaptive intelligence".

In this book I want to explore what this means for the way we learn in the real world. Our ancestors developed physical tools – axes, fire, wheels, buildings, printing presses and so on. We need to develop a correspondingly helpful set of mental tools or mindware to ensure that we cope with the new circumstances in which we find ourselves. Faced with virtually no time to process new challenges and new ways of doing things, how best should we react? To thrive in the first part of the twenty-first century requires some new rules (as well as a fresh look at some old ones).

We are, I will argue, in the middle of a revolution with a small "r". A *rEvolution* if you like. Some of the traditional ways of approaching things still work well, while others need to be turned on their head. And in some cases we simply need fresh ways of looking at what is happening around us.

Adaptive intelligence

Developing adaptive expertise involves some fundamental rethinking about intelligence. This will express itself in two ways; in the habits of mind[1] we cultivate in our daily lives and in the patterns of social interaction we choose with other human beings.

Where once smart people knew a lot of stuff and were confident that their way of doing things was the most enlightened, we may need to get better at unlearning things and at managing short-term relationships.

If it was a safe bet to do more of the same or simply try harder, it may be more helpful to understand the processes of habit and change the ways in which we can harness the energy of those around us to help us stick to any new resolve.

Where in the past we spent our time in forensic analysis and problem-solving we may prefer to shift our attention to appreciative inquiry and to the formation of richly rewarding reciprocal relationships with other like-minded people.

And, while the lessons of history will continue to be valuable, we may become more suspicious of traditional "experience" as we go into uncharted waters and look as well for the capacity to imagine futures, to reframe situations and to conduct, with others, a series of ongoing experiments into the way we live our lives.

---

[1] Throughout the book I use the phrase "habits of mind" (as used by Arthur Costa and Bena Kallick in an educational context – www.habits-of-mind.net) to describe the kinds of adaptive dispositions I am suggesting.

Whether ideas like these seem like revolution or evolution will probably depend on your state of mind and personal knowledge and experience. *rEvolution: How to Thrive in Crazy Times* is not a traditional self-help guide. Rather it is aimed at anyone who is curious enough to pull it down from the bookshelf hoping for a more eclectic and wider-ranging selection of ideas than is traditional in many of these kinds of books. Some of the suggestions will be familiar to readers. But in the blending of the known and the unknown I hope you will find useful prompts to action or at least be stirred to find out more about something that has reawakened your interest. If you are working in organisations you may find yourself part of a "change programme" and be grateful for the orientation a book like this can give you. And in your role as citizen of a changing world I hope that something I have written may gently nudge you into further reading, contemplation or action.

A brief history of change

Let me go back in time for a moment to put Darwin and other evolutionary thinking in context.

For a few billion years there were just single-celled organisms on earth. Then our immediate ape-like ancestors emerged from the swamp. And, somewhere between a hundred thousand and a million years ago, Homo sapiens "arrived". These are the slow and fascinating processes of natural selection described by Charles Darwin.

Then, as an intelligent species, we invented tools, fire, language, farming and civilised living. A few centuries ago we started to get clever with machines, harnessing the power of water, steam, gas, oil and electricity. We learned how to communicate in print, how to travel around the globe at speed and, only decades ago, we invented the computer and the World Wide Web. Most of these changes took a long time, many centuries or at least decades.

But the latest kinds of computer-driven evolution use a much tighter timescale. They operate in years, months or days. For just as we have automated production in much of our living, so with new computer science there is a sense in which we are beginning to automate evolution. Avoiding the debate as to whether computers will render us redundant (personally I do not believe that they will) they will undoubtedly be able to do things that we cannot. They can already recognise patterns, relatively quickly, which we cannot discern. (We can see this, for example, in the recent advances in our understanding of both climate change and of the human genome.) They can learn behaviour, continuously reprogramming themselves to do things more effectively. They can bring massive amounts of data to bear on complex problems in ways in which the human mind cannot. And in case you think I am only interested in "Homo technians", I am not. Almost every aspect of human inventiveness is being challenged today.

Once evolution was in nature's random, slow and playful hands. Now it is in our own. It is increasingly fast with the possibility that new evolutions can almost immediately be spread through the World Wide Web. In this book I will explore not the moral or other purposes to which human beings may direct the evolution of our species but the ways in which we may like to adapt our minds to whatever happens.

Different kinds of change

Of course change arrives in many forms:

- *Good and bad.* There's change which is good such as a new cure for an old disease. Or a similar technology may be turned into a biological weapon.

- *Significant or minor.* We alter a deeply engrained pattern of behaviour or we move the furniture around in our living room or buy a new mobile phone.

- *Personal or social.* A new child is born or the well-being and lives of thousands of people are affected by a natural disaster.

- *Desired or not.* There's change that we want such as a new partner, a new job or a new belief. Or there are the changes that are forced upon us which we may not desire at all: separation, death, redundancy and loss of faith are the flip side of the coin.

And within these categories there are at least three degrees of impact.

First there are all the hundreds of minor *reorderings* we undergo on a daily basis – a new look or hairstyle, a new gadget or a different route to work.

Then there are more significant developments, the *real-world adaptations* that we undertake either consciously or not. We finally give up a smoking habit, we stop taking short-haul flights and travel by train, we start playing a musical instrument or join a gym.

And finally the third level – the most difficult to navigate – a major *reprogramming*, either sought, achieved or experienced accidentally, such as a fundamental reappraisal of your working life, moving from employed to self-employed status or the loss of a lifelong and much loved spouse.

The poetry and philosophy of change

Perhaps, not surprisingly, when life moves along more slowly it tends to be poets and philosophers who spend time thinking about change, often by speculating about what is permanent and what is changeable in life. Shakespeare's

Seven Ages of Man speech in *As You Like It* is, perhaps, the purest example of this:

> All the world's a stage,
> And all the men and women merely players;
> They have their exits and their entrances,
> And one man in his time plays many parts,
> His acts being seven ages. At first, the infant,
> Mewling and puking in the nurse's arms.
> Then the whining schoolboy, with his satchel
> And shining morning face, creeping like snail
> Unwillingly to school. And then the lover,
> Sighing like furnace, with a woeful ballad
> Made to his mistress' eyebrow. Then a soldier,
> Full of strange oaths and bearded like the pard,
> Jealous in honour, sudden and quick in quarrel,
> Seeking the bubble reputation
> Even in the canon's mouth. And then the justice,
> In fair round belly with good capon lined,
> With eyes severe and beard of formal cut,
> Full of wise saws and modern instances;
> And so he plays his part. The sixth age shifts
> Into the lean and slippered pantaloon
> With spectacles on nose and pouch on side;
> His youthful hose, well saved, a world too wide
> For his shrunk shank, and his big manly voice,
> Turning again toward childish treble, pipes
> And whistles in his sound. Last scene of all,
> That ends this strange eventful history,
> Is second childishness and mere oblivion,
> Sans teeth, sans eyes, sans taste, sans everything.

Where poets remark on the passage of the seasons and the ageing process, philosophers speculate on the essence of change, wondering about the notion of fixity and permanence. Greek thinkers famously waxed lyrical on the subject some two and a half thousand years ago. Heraclitus, with startling prescience, argued that the only constant was change itself. As a consequence we can never drink from the same river twice because, although it may look similar, it is in fact different.

By contrast, Empedocles saw the world as made of the elements of fire, air, water and earth, only changing as the consequence of one of two forces: "love/harmony" or "hatred/strife". In his world view the four elements are the fixed components while their impact on us changes according to the positive or negative forces of love or hatred.

Both Heraclitus and Empedocles, in trying to account for change, end up by defining it in terms of the permanent elements which they favour. The exception to this is arguably Parmenides who seems to argue that there is no such thing as change. While things may appear to change, their underlying reality remains constant and indestructible.

In an echo of Empedocles, the great Chinese philosophers sought to define the workings of the world in the *Book of Changes*. They called this the Tao or "workings of the universe". From this they derived yin and yang, the two opposing forces which, as with Empedocles' love and hatred, shape the world, often in cyclical fashion.

Yin and yang are used to account for all change. And all change can be explained by yin, yang and five agents – earth, fire, metal, wood and water. At their simplest levels, yin is associated with femaleness, the moon, completion, cold, darkness, wetness and passivity, while yang is maleness, the sun, creation, heat, light, Heaven, dryness and dominance.

Yin and yang help to ensure an endless cycle of change, with neither dominating. Each depends on the other; each, in a sense, causes the other. And, in this world view, any condition – sickness or health, happiness or misery, good or bad government – is explicable by reference to yin or yang. The action of yin and yang on the matter that makes up our world accounts for and explains everything in the world that changes.

Precisely because we cannot see what goes on within ourselves or beneath the surface of the world about us, exactly what underpins the changes we all experience has been a source of much speculation for many centuries. Not surprisingly we have sought to account for change by imposing our own theoretical frameworks on it. A good example of this is the Hippocratic idea of the four humours – blood, phlegm, black bile and yellow bile. Each of these had associations with different elements and suggested certain temperamental tendencies:

- Blood, associated with *air*, became synonymous with sanguine (from the Latin *sanguineus*).

- Phlegm, linked to *water* and calm, becomes phlegmatic.

- Black bile, connected to the element *earth*, gave rise to melancholia and being melancholic via the Greek for "black" (μελας) and "cholic" (χολη).

- Yellow bile, like *fire*, indicates energy and passion and is summed up by the word choleric.

As with the four elements of Empedocles, the four humours provide a way of explaining change and exploring the idea of what it is to be living a life which is in balance. If you have an excess of yellow bile, you may blaze away and be exhausting to be with; if too much black bile, then you may be prone to depressive reactions to the cruelty and unfairness of life. And so on.

These ideas found rich roots in medieval medicine and science so that they emerge almost unscathed at the end of the nineteenth century as the first great psychologists were using more scientific methods to account for the way we all grow and change. Carl Jung's theory of personality, later adapted into what is now known as the MBTI (Myers-Briggs Type Indicator) by the Myers-Briggs sisters, still betrays our hunger for dynamic frameworks, by which I mean for ways of seeing ourselves as in the middle of opposing forces.

The MBTI mines this idea by applying it to four key human activities which, taken together, go to make up personality:

1. Source of energy – the degree to which you look externally or socially for your energy as opposed to preferring a more inward and reflective attitude.

2. Information-gathering – how concrete (noticed by your five senses) or intuitive (abstract, intuitive) you tend to be.

3. Decision-making – the tension between rational and emotional thought.

4. Lifestyle orientation – perhaps the element accounting for the greatest source of tension within people, the degree to which you favour an ordered and predictable world or one more flexible, open-ended and fluid.

Later on we will explore the degree to which some people may find it easier to change, for example if they are temperamentally more likely to be open to new and unplanned experiences.

The stirrings of science

It was not only philosophers and psychologists who were keen to account for change. Astronomers and astrologists have also exerted much influence. Astronomy, the oldest of the sciences, turned to the heavens to find patterns and to track celestial movement. But at the same time as the astronomical eye looked to the sky the human mind made connections with earthly events – fire, pestilence, the birth of a great saviour. It also marvelled at the grandeur and power of what it saw with the naked eye or through the telescope and assumed some kind of divine role.

The earth's movement around the sun (albeit initially thought to be the other way round) gave us the basis for the measure of all change, the yearly calendar. But then the astrologers got their hands on things. A science became a pseudoscience. While Nostradamus may be a name we know, the reliability of his predictions was extremely limited. The astrologer's tendency to cede human free will to the movement of the stars, combined with the deep instinctive love for shamans that seems to exist in many of us, created an industry that still thrives today. Newspapers and websites have found horoscopes to be powerfully enticing, giving millions of people daily plausible enough predictions of the changing circumstances of their lives. In fact, it never ceases to amaze me that otherwise intelligent and sane members of the human race still seem to want to see what fate allegedly has in store for them!

But, as I have already suggested, it is the scientist, Charles Darwin, who, some one hundred and fifty years ago, arguably gave us the most potent theory of change. His theory of natural selection accounts for the gradual improvement of the various species which inhabit a crowded planet. At its heart is a simple but powerful idea that it is not the strongest or most intelligent of the species that survive but those that are the most adaptable to change.

In other words, things change not because of a dynamic tension between elements (as with earlier Greek or Chinese views) but because of a complex and, in most cases, rather slow series of modifications and developments which play out over time. As a consequence certain species thrive where others do not. And within species, modifications occur which more effectively suit the external environment and so get passed down the generations.

Darwin, especially with the benefit of recent advances in our understanding of the human genome, helps us to understand why human beings have so much in common with other species. But he does not account for why we, as a species, are actually so *different* from other species, and why, as I am arguing in *rEvolution*, our minds are running away with us so fast that change which was once so gradual is now so rapid.

In recent years there have been two powerful attempts to account for human evolution. The first, by Richard Dawkins, in his book *The Selfish Gene*, looks to the genes themselves for the explanation. Genes, he argues, are self-ish. They have to be. For their job is survival by any means. However this does not mean that in the way we behave we necessarily need to be cold and cunning to thrive. In fact, in a chapter called "Nice guys finish first" Dawkins demonstrates, through game theory and symbiotic examples from the natural world, how the smart response is often to act collectively not competitively.

In *The Meme Machine*, Susan Blackmore goes one stage further. Rather than focusing on genes, she explores the "meme", a concept first coined by Richard Dawkins. A meme is the cultural equivalent to a gene. So memes are ideas, new words, new fashions, new inventions, new ways of doing the high-jump or different ways of doing the complex mathematics and science of, say, climate change, which transmit themselves from one mind to another. The successful memes are the ones that last.

Blackmore elegantly explores the ways in which memes account for those aspects of human evolution on which Darwin has *least* to say, all the things to do with language, ideas and culture. The central thesis is that a unique element of our makeup is our ability to imitate. Blackmore extends this to show how the evolutionary journey human beings are engaged upon is a different kind of selection, not so much natural as cultural. In this new evolutionary soup it is ideas which compete for space in our minds.

And Blackmore goes one step further, making a case for a genuinely different approach to the way humans change by invoking the possibility that even our non-conscious self (or indeed consciousness itself) are illusions created by our memes. In this she is drawing in part on the fascinating notion of adaptive self-deception first advanced by Robert Trivers.

Think about it like this. If any particular human being is really to be ultimately successful then there will be times when he or she will not want to betray feelings to an enemy, for by detecting fear the enemy might sense an advantage. So what more cunning way of ensuring survival could there be than for an individual to be genuinely unaware of things which might otherwise be transmitted to their opponent!

Darwin's concept of evolution and his subsequent elaborators changed our view of the world dramatically, just as Nicholas Copernicus did when he placed the sun at the centre of our universe or as Christopher Columbus and other notable round-the-world sailors achieved with their safe return home with regard to the idea of a flat earth.

These moments are what Thomas Kuhn, in *The Structure of Scientific Revolutions*, called "paradigm shifts", moments when there is a significant change in our basic assumptions about the way the world works.

Personal and social change

So far we have touched on just a few of the big philosophical and scientific approaches to change in a loosely historical sort of a way. Of course, no one strand of thinking is discrete as we found when moving from Greek philosophy to contemporary psychology via medieval medicine. In this section I want to look briefly at some more socio-cultural lines of thinking.

One trend is very clear. Where once thinkers, from whatever discipline, tended to look for single causes today we are looking at the world as a complex adaptive system with no simple control levers. Good examples of complex adaptive systems are the international banking system (as revealed in the sub-prime mortgage shocks which rippled their way around the globe in 2007–8), the world's weather, a flock of birds on the wing, a jazz band in full music-making mode, human beings and, of course, the human mind.

If this seems complex and as yet impractical, then that's probably because it is! As Douglas Adams put it in *The Restaurant at the End of the Universe*: "There is a theory which states that if ever anyone discovers exactly what the Universe is for and why it is here, it will instantly disappear and be replaced by something even more bizarre and inexplicable. There is another theory which states that this has already happened."

Personal power

Empedocles. Copernicus. Darwin. Kuhn. This litany of names reminds us of how much changing world views are associated with individual thinkers. But there is another view, well expressed by Willis Harman: "Throughout history, the really fundamental changes in society have come about not from the dictates of governments and the results of battles but through vast numbers of people changing their minds – sometimes only a little bit." I will return both to the significant roles we as individuals can all play in times of change and to the idea of changing minds.

It is worth remembering that, for some while, we thought that human beings were largely victims of the circumstances of their environment. Pavlov's dogs salivated when bells were rung because they were always fed when the bell was rung. Skinner's rats responded to cues in their environment. Unsurprisingly they modified their activity according to rewards and sanctions. And such changes somehow persuaded us that environment was a more powerful influence on our behaviours than our own determined intentions. Thus behaviourism was born and its ideas held sway for many decades.

Until that is, in the 1980s, when significant new thinking about the power of mindset began to challenge more deterministic views of human behaviour. At least two fruitful lines of enquiry emerged. One, often referred to as positive psychology, is closely associated with the work of Martin Seligman. For Seligman, especially with his idea of "learned optimism", reminds us that change is not an absolute concept. It is perfectly possible for different people to view the same event through very different lenses. For one individual life seems good while for another everything is going wrong.

The second line of thought also qualifies events through the lens of an individual's personal perception. Change happens, but, as Carol Dweck has shown, its impact on us varies according to our mindset. If we believe that we have the potential to grow and develop, then change is to be welcomed. We will rise to the challenge. Whereas if we have a fixed sense of our own talents, then change becomes much more threatening for we may not have what it takes to deal with it. "People's ideas about risk and effort grow out of their basic mindset," Dweck reminds us. If we believe that we can, through our own efforts, rise to new heights, then change is a challenge and we are happy to take risks. Whereas, if we have a fixed mindset then change is an unwelcome test of our ability, one which we may not wish to explore for fear of failure or of not coming up to the mark.

One of the most influential metaphors for imagining change was created by physicist turned social scientist Kurt Lewin in the first part of the twentieth century. His three stage model involves unfreezing, changing, then refreezing. Unfreezing is the process by which existing ideas, beliefs, habits or ways of doing things are dismantled. Then there is an uncertain time – the *crazy times* – suggested by the subtitle of this book. This most difficult period is followed by the third stage during which new patterns are established and embedded.

Changing behaviour is here being compared to the way in which you might refashion a square block of ice into a new shape, say a doughnut. It would be impossible to chip away at the cube and reform it into a pristine tyre shape. The only means of achieving this would be to turn the ice into water, pour it into a new mould and refreeze it. The metaphor has resonance at many levels – personal, social and societal. Most importantly it reminds us that there is essentially a transition between two fixed states. For many people today, with so much change in the air, it is difficult to imagine what fixed new state to aim for. Not surprisingly, life is stressful, crazy, even. There are, however, many ways of getting better at dealing with change, as we shall discover, at home and at work.

Most recently it has begun to occur to many people that, with the increasing power of computers and computer-driven technology, we may be on the verge of a new kind of evolution. James Martin puts this most compellingly when he talks of three eras of evolution. The first was the slow process of natural selection, so brilliantly described by Darwin, which culminated in the arrival of Homo sapiens. The second phase, about which Darwin had little or nothing to say specifically, was the period during which Homo sapiens used his intelligence to develop ideas, inventions, machines, tools and so on. This is where we are today and the difference between the first two phases is that where once evolution was in nature's hands, now it is in ours.

Commentators like Martin speculate that we are now standing on the edge of a third kind of evolution which is automated. In this brave new world two things happen. First, the speed of change increases exponentially and, second, our control of the evolutionary process passes more and more to smart machines. For computers increasingly are able to see patterns that human beings simply cannot see (think of the human genome or Google) by coping with huge amounts of data. They can also learn adaptive behaviours by using sophisticated feedback loops and predictive software. This "evolutionary engineering" is increasingly very, very fast and spread via the Internet. During this third period Homo sapiens will be faced with some stark choices at the heart of which will be a question about the degree to which we want to use some of the technology we have created to live longer and use manufactured components which will prolong life way beyond the timescales attributable to biological evolution.

In this brief history of evolution we have touched on just a few lines of thinking about how and why human beings have changed into what we are today. Throughout *rEvolution* we will be exploring aspects of this kind of thinking in more detail, asking ourselves a repeated question, "So what?" What does it mean for us today and what might we do differently as a consequence? How can we stay sane in difficult times? These are big questions to which in many cases we are only just beginning to formulate answers.

As Richard Dawkins puts it:

After sleeping through a hundred million centuries we have finally opened our eyes on a sumptuous planet, sparkling with colour, bountiful with life. Within decades we must close our eyes again. Isn't it a noble, an enlightened way of spending our brief time in the sun, to work at understanding the universe and how we have come to wake up in it? This is how I answer when I am asked – as I am surprisingly often – why I bother to get up in the mornings.

Rule 1 – Change is changing

Whosoever desires constant success must change his conduct with the times.

Niccolò Machiavelli

Crazy times

God give us grace to accept with serenity the things that cannot be changed, courage to change the things which should be changed and the wisdom to distinguish the one from the other.

Reinhold Niebuhr

Nothing stays the same for long. The sun goes in. We get sick. Children grow up. Our hips fall apart. Winter comes. We fall in love. We fall out of love. We buy a new car. We find faith. A cherished belief is challenged. We go to the moon. We discover the human genome. Computers get smarter. Seeds become plants, bloom, die and return to the earth.

We know all this stuff. We're experts. We've been dealing with this kind of change ever since we were born. That's why we are still alive. It's why human beings rule the planet.

But hold on. Are we so confident? Or is there something different going on right now?

Some forty years ago Alvin Toffler warned us that something strange was happening. He called it future shock, "the shattering stress and disorientation that we induce in individuals by subjecting them to too much change in too short a time". In these crazy times the tempo of life has become so rapid that we no longer have time to process our responses to what is going on around us.

For many people this means feeling constantly on the back foot, warding off some new attack. At home, parents struggle to comprehend their children's online social networking activities and grandparents find themselves suddenly called upon to be child minders just when they had hoped to have some time for themselves. Businesses uproot aspects of their work to other parts of the globe at the drop of a corporate hat. And ubiquitous hand-held devices mean that some people are never alone, constantly carrying on multiple conversations with work colleagues and family members even as they purport to be attending to other activities around them. Change is 24/7. Change is remorseless. As a consequence of this many people feel fearful, bewildered and stressed out.

Until quite recently it was a reasonable assumption to make that change takes time and is fundamentally a gradual process. Even Moore's Law, the technological one about the speed of computers doubling every eighteen months, while scary, seems somehow manageable. Eighteen months is a long time, we think to ourselves. I'll be a whole year older. Nothing to panic about. But if this law continues to hold fast (which some doubt), in just fifteen years computers will be a thousand times faster than now and capable of doing things which most of us have not even begun to dream about.

The first rule of *rEvolution* is this: change is changing. And some change is so fast that, if we want to survive, we need to evolve a different way of dealing with change, understanding more about whether it is good or bad, radical or minor, personal or social, desirable or not, and so on.

Inside the human mind

Driving our evolution is, of course, the human mind. And here there is an interesting tension – for our very survival has depended on two forces which lead us to react to change in very different ways. On the one hand our minds are wonderfully curious, endlessly seeking out new experiences. We want to see if the world really is flat or if it is possible to land on Mars or crash small particles together to understand more about how the universe began. We enjoy visiting new places, meeting new friends, taking on new challenges. We are constantly coming up with new inventions, new words, new ways of doing things. In short, just as our brain is constructed of billions of neurons which connect together to enable us to function, so our minds thrive on making connections.

Our brain is so good at making connections that it will even fill in the gaps when it is missing information. Watch a cat moving along behind a fence and although part of the cat's body is obscured behind the posts of the fence, you will still think that you are seeing a whole cat! As the poet Robert Frost put it, "an idea is a feat of association". We thrive by taking knowledge we have acquired in one domain of our life and applying it in another context, and metaphors often provide the mental springboard between situations (as with the ice idea we were playing with in the Introduction). And our use of language is critically important as we will see later on. Indeed the full Frost quotation reads: "An idea is a feat of association, and the height of it is a good metaphor."

But an equally powerful aspect of the human mind is its ability to create patterns out of experience. If our exploring minds provide us with our energy for change and evolution, our pattern-making mind helps us to stay sane by making sense of the huge amount of data which we experience on a daily basis. If we did not have this faculty we would go stir-crazy! So words get formed into sentences, dictionaries, novels and screenplays. Places get named, linked by roads and before we know it, Google Earth is born. Civilisation is born out of our pattern-making minds. We create homes, streets, villages, towns, cities and global entities such as the World Wide Web. We make order out of chaos.

Human beings could not have survived without our ability to pattern-match; without it, at its simplest level, we would have long ago been eaten by predators. If you have never seen a lion, then the first time you see one you may think it is a horse (four legs, brown coat and a mane). Indeed one has to presume that some of our ancestors were eaten by lions until they learned more accurately to spot the distinctive size, colour, shape and sound of a lion and file it in the part of the brain labelled "dangerous animals". A similar argument can be made for all the plants which we now know to be poisonous. Indeed, at one level, all learning and all evolutionary adaptation is a kind of pattern-matching. We find ourselves in a new situation and, often unconsciously, a question fires up in our brain: "Where have I seen one of these before?" A colleague starts to get angry in a meeting and we dimly recall that the last time we responded in similarly angry vein the meeting went badly wrong. At the same time another thought emerges in our mind providing us with a different pattern, a memory of a similar situation in which anger was met with empathy and humour leading to a more positive outcome, and we decide to use the second and more sophisticated of these two strategies. We have learned, adapted and evolved as a person as a consequence.

These two aspects of our mindware – exploring and pattern-making – both serve us well. But each brings with it some clues as to why dealing with change can be difficult. Consider this image. Can you see a woman at the window?

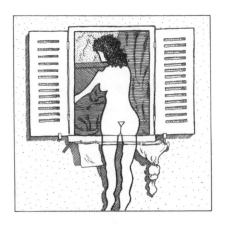

Most people can. But look again. There is no woman. Sure there is a cat and above the cat there is a shelf with a pot plant. To the right there is a curtain. That is a wine glass not a finely turned pair of buttocks! And as to those being legs, they are in fact just various articles of underwear happily swinging in the warm sunshine.

At the rational level there is no woman at the window. But can you still see one? Most people can. In other words, our pattern-making mind can be too clever for its own good. Once we have come to a conclusion we can be very loath to give it up, even if there is direct evidence to the contrary. We will need to remember this when we are exploring ways of dealing with change later on.

"The woman at the window" provides a metaphor for many of the choices we make in our real lives. So, even though we know it would be better for the planet if we cycled to work and better for our health if we walked, we still persist in taking the car and driving a mile down the road. Whether we are dealing with longstanding habits or ways of seeing the world which are only seconds old (as with the woman at the window), habits (or patterns) easily become engrained so that it becomes unhelpfully difficult to change them.

A trivial example that makes the point is the way we fold our arms. Stand up for a moment and fold your arms. Chances are you have folded them in the way that you normally fold them. Try folding them the other way. Some people find this a surprisingly hard task. Whereas the first way was easy, the second is a bit of a palaver. For a moment help has to be sought from the conscious mind to issue commands to hands and elbows to meld themselves into the unaccustomed shape. Practise the unfamiliar arm-crossing a few times and it seems much easier. Out of habit most of us only fold our arms one way. For when we grow weary of the one way, we let our arms drop to our sides. Then when we feel like folding them we adopt our familiar right over left or left over right habit. Sometimes in r*Evolution* I will be asking you to consider "folding your arms the other way"!

Or what about this old chestnut, as reinvented by The Mind Gym. Which line is longer?

They are both the same, I hear you mutter. Not so. You have been tricked. Turn the page and look at it again.

As you can see the top line is in fact noticeably longer. Sceptical readers may at this moment want to use a ruler to check that there has been no trickery! In this simple moment something else about the human mind reveals itself – its astonishing smugness! Fooled once by a non-existent woman we are quick to reassert our rational vigour!

We will see how answers to longstanding problems change over time and how people who are likely to thrive in changing times remain open to reassessing data before simply giving a pat response.

The astonishing pace of change

Alvin Toffler was right when he argued that: "the accelerative thrust triggered by man has become the key to the entire evolutionary process on the planet". These are the crazy times we live in. After many years in caves, mankind has latterly showed his devastating brilliance and is accelerating into an uncertain future. Today we can do something new and in seconds it has travelled around the world via the

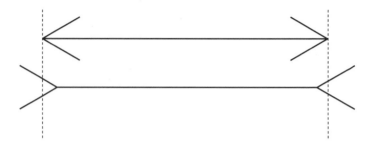

Internet. Homes are changing, work is changing, computer-aided living is moving on in leaps and bounds. We are surrounded by such a dazzling array of things to choose from, whether we think of phones, television channels, low-cost flights, even brands of coffee! For growing numbers of people there is no longer such a thing as a routine day or routine week.

For some time we have had multiple identities, typically combining parent, earner and any role we may have in the community. But the money earning element of this equation has become increasingly less straightforward. Increasing numbers of people, like me, live portfolio lives. In my case this means combining writing, speaking, facilitating and researching for a range of very different clients. The idea of a career is fast becoming obsolete. Even if you start out on one (as I did becoming a teacher) there is a significant chance that you will change your employment path subsequently (as I have done making two separate shifts, first into the third sector and currently into the for-profit world where I run my own business).

I no longer have a job-shaped job and am unemployable in the conventional sense of that word. Significant changes have been built in to my employment trajectory. Ten years ago I might have felt different from many of my friends. But now at least half of them have similarly complex lives. There are going to be fewer and fewer job-shaped jobs; soon, portfolio lives with multiple identities will be the norm for many people and at far earlier stages in their lives.

The consequence of living in crazy times

You have been patient while I have sketched out, as it were, the history of our crazy times. My purpose has been to argue that change itself is changing and to understand how the emerging sciences of evolution and change are so multilayered and complex. Where once, as Darwin showed us, it was a slow and random process of adaptation, today it is much faster, more conscious and more obviously influenced by human beings.

In short there is no such thing as a routine any more. In the past we expected periods of relative stability and cycles of life which we could measure in generations or at least years, today life comes at us in a rush. Where routines exist still they are likely to be in those domestic areas of our life where we have most control (what we do when we get up, our route to school if we are a child, the way we organise our domestic lives if we live with others under one roof).

Leave the confines of home and, whether it is booking a holiday, communicating with our friends or making choices about how we get our news or information about the world, we have more choices than ever. "Our brain", as neurologist Richard Restak has suggested, "is being forced to manage increasing amounts of information." In crazy times of rapid change we will all need to become better at dealing with huge amounts of information and at extracting the meaning out of our experiences. And this calls for some different priorities. As Eric Hoffer memorably put it: "In times of change learners inherit the earth; while the learned find themselves beautifully equipped to deal with a world that no longer exists."

The new mindware

In this Rule (and in all of the subsequent Rules), I want to suggest some of the ways in which we might want to focus our effort. But first a thought about language. As Stephen Pinker reminds us so eloquently, human beings are "ver-bivores" a species that lives "on" words and enjoys explor-ing the meanings they convey. Today it is "Google" and "Blackberry" in the ascendancy and few now use a phrase like "the information superhighway" which for a brief time was in vogue. Another candidate for a word that has possi-bly outlived its usefulness is "skill", for it emerged from an era when things moved more slowly. We knew what skills were required to do most jobs and they could be learned through apprenticeship. We knew which skills we had to learn at school because they were enmeshed either in the 3Rs of reading, writing and arithmetic or in the predictable subjects of school – Geography, French, Woodwork and so on.

These days we need more than skills. We need skills in action or as I will call them, adopting the phrase popu-larised by Art Costa and Bena Kallick in the US, "habits of mind". It's no good if our skills are theoretical only and too "rusty" from lack of use to rely on when we need them. One essential habit of mind we need, paradoxically, is being able to unlearn things. (Remember the woman at the window and the two lines puzzle which both showed how easily we can become fixed in our view of the world!) We also need to be able to transfer learning from one part of our life and apply it another area. And frequently our learning will be social, involving highly developed approaches to collabora-tion and reciprocal living.

There are two kinds of mindware that I will be exploring here and throughout *rEvolution*:

1. The personal habits of mind that are most conducive to the set of challenges outlined in each Rule.

2. The patterns of social interaction – how we go about our relationships with the other members of our "tribe".

Habits of mind and patterns of action

If we want to thrive in crazy times, we may like to get better at imagining, noticing, choosing, synthesising and, perhaps most fundamentally, unlearning.

While in terms of the patterns of interaction we need to adopt, I start *rEvolution* as I end it, with explicit advocacy of collaborative living and learning, or what I am calling "socialising with intent". Here I will explore ideas of social capital, social intuition and systems thinking, and suggest ways in which the way we build up our experience bank and contact network is likely to influence our success in life.

Imagining

At one level the faster the world turns, the more imagining (as opposed to doing) can seem a waste of time. And the following apocryphal exchange from a school classroom makes clear just how embedded is the idea of the wastefulness of human effort:

> Teacher: What are you doing? *(Pupil is looking out of the window)*
> Child: Imagining, thinking, Miss.
> Teacher: Well get on with your work, then!

Daydreaming can be helpful or wasteful. Sometimes it helps us to recharge ourselves and rethink something without focusing so hard that we get stuck. But unless we have the ability to create in our mind's eye something that is not there and to view it from different perspectives, then it is very difficult to see how we can visualise the future.

Increasingly we will need a combination of many disciplines to help us. But a common strand is likely to be our ability to visualise. Indeed, while of course it will always be helpful to use history and study the lessons of the past, as we move into uncharted territory we will need to be able to call on ways of using our mind which seek to adapt existing knowledge to new circumstances. This new discipline will be multi-disciplinary. Take this well-known example of what is sometimes called geometric growth to make my point. Earlier I mentioned Moore's Law about computer power doubling every eighteen months. If you just rely on mathematics, this may remain a relatively abstract concept. But add in some biology and a bit of creative visualisation and suddenly your ability to envisage the future can come alive.

Imagine you have a pond in your garden. For years its surface is completely clear and you enjoy the sight of tadpoles and dragonflies throughout its annual cycle. But one day a duck stops off to search for food before heading off for the river nearby. On its feet it carries tiny bits of pond weed. Imagine that duckweed follows a pattern of geometric growth like computer power and, to keep it simple, that it doubles in size every day. Now look at the sequence of pictures below which chart the last week of your pond's life before it becomes completely choked with weed.

For many days prior to this, potentially for many months, if someone told you that your pond was shortly to be completely covered with weed you might have scoffed at them, telling them to mind their own business. Unless, that is, you had a tendency to visualise abstract ideas!

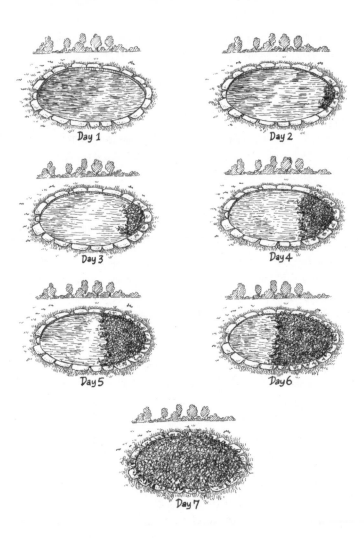

Noticing

Closely allied to imagining is our ability to *notice*. For at some stage, still using the pond example, you would have had to notice either the surprise visit of a duck or the first traces of weed in your pond. More than this you would have had to make some connections in your own mind between these events so that, while there was only a very small area of weed you did your best to remove every trace you could.

Another watery example is sometimes quoted to illustrate the dangers of not noticing – the sad story of the boiled frog. It goes like this. If you put a frog in a beaker of water and gradually heat the water the frog will not notice. Eventually it will boil to death. Or so the story goes. This is an example of exactly the kind of apocryphal tale that gains credence on the Internet, if unchallenged. (See Rule 7 for more on the importance of real searching!) In fact it turns out, on closer exploration of the science, that any self-respecting frog would become increasingly agitated and use its long legs to hop out of the water unless the beaker was very high-sided. But even this discredited story makes a useful point: it is a precondition of dealing with any chance effectively that you need to have ways of noticing when the heat is on.

It is very easy to see (or hear) without noticing and, in particular, without seeing the connections between things and their underlying patterns. This is the kind of noticing that leads to understanding. Sometimes it exists at the rational level. We notice that a parent's reaction times have slowed down to such an extent that we conclude that the time has come for them to stop driving a car. Often it is more tentative. We have a gut feel that something is not quite right with a friend but can't quite put our finger on what it is. Then gradually we begin to connect this intuitive sense with other observable details – an occasional late arrival, a slightly more dishevelled look than normal. And from these noticings we resolve to talk more and find out what lies beneath them. More contemporary examples might be to do with the impact of excessive computer gaming on a teenager or the effect of one person's Blackberry dependence on an adult relationship. In all these examples the noticing needs to be more than casual if it is to be effective in spotting trends and seeing underlying patterns. Later on we will explore the social implications of more systemic noticing, what happens when a hunch is surfaced and becomes a tentative assumption.

Tool – The Five Whys

A simple tool which can help in making our noticing more effective is the Five Whys. Credited to car manufacturer Toyota, the Five Whys tend to encourage a certain kind of enquiring mind. It encourages users to look beyond mere symptoms to underlying causes and potential trends. To take a simple example, let's suppose that you are consistently late for work. Your Five Whys in answer to the initial question of, say, "Why are you late for work?" might develop like this:

1. Why? I got up too late.

2. Why? I went to bed too late.

3. Why? I drank too much wine.

4. Why? I am working too hard.

5. Why? I am unhappy at work.

When you habitually explore your noticings with a pattern of consecutive questioning like this – each more probing than the one before – the trends behind apparently insignificant occurrences can become clearer. Of course in today's fast-changing world, the notion of being late for work may, itself, be anachronistic soon!

Choosing

As human innovation flourishes, so too does the proliferation of products available to us to enrich our lives. On the one hand this is further testimony to the success of human evolution. Go to any supermarket and you can see how clever we have become. No longer do we just select either gold top or ordinary milk, we will find many different kinds of milk, from cows, from soya beans, from rice; some with additives like vitamins or fish oil; some organic, some farm assured, some just "cheap". And this level of complexity is replicated if you are looking for coffee, jam, cereal or anything else you might want to buy. Of course, it also occurs in a parallel world of online shopping. Here, assuming you are wanting non-perishable goods, you don't just have a choice between real and virtual shops, you can also consider the merits of new or second-hand, courtesy of the eBay revolution.

The same situation exists with regard to watching television or listening to music. Where once there was a simple matter of choosing between three or four competing programmes in an evening, now choice is unlimited. You can potentially watch anything whenever you want to. Similarly with music. No longer is the boundary of your listening choice determined by the stack of records, tapes or latterly CDs, because you are only one click away from an almost infinite global music store. This proliferation is evident in most aspects of modern living. In short, we are spoilt for choice in almost every aspect of our lives.

Far from enriching our lives, psychologists have shown that too much choice makes us unhappy in a variety of different experimental contexts. We actually end up buying less and doing less well. Some fifty years ago, in a seminal paper with the intriguing title "The Magical Number Seven, Plus or Minus Two: Some Limits On Our Capacity For Processing Information", cognitive psychologist George

Miller explained why there is a limit to the capacity of human beings to process data. Essentially the working memory of a typical human brain can deal with up to about seven items at any one time. Faced with choosing from a shelf stacked with twenty or thirty products we are not, in any real sense of the word, able to "choose". There's just too much data to process.

So, while it may be a sign of progress that we are capable of so much invention, if we want to stay sane we may want to narrow this down somewhat in our daily lives. Sometimes our lives are made easier in this regard by technology. Online retailers Amazon make it easier for me to choose by telling me that "Customers Who Bought Items Like This Also Bought ...". Computers encourage us to add websites we like to our "Favourites". Online retailers store our last order so that we are not starting from scratch each time we start to shop. MP3 players can be used intelligently to allow us to listen to the music we have already chosen or simply be set to play a random selection and relieve us of the burden of choice. Increasingly, smart digital recording machines "know" our preferences and record things they think we may enjoy. By the same token the Google function offers us so much choice that it can easily itself act as a bewildering rather than an enabling technology.

But really what we need to do involves a shift in mindset. Provided we are not fazed by the knowledge that we have more recorded programmes than we could ever make time to watch, we are not harmed by such a treasure trove of stored delights. As digital memory fills up content can simply be deleted (as it can always be downloaded at a later stage). It is a only a problem if the unused material begins to weigh on our mind, like a stack of unread novels or non-fiction texts waiting on a shelf for that elusive long summer holiday break that, in our busy lives, we never have time to take! What we really need to do is consciously to reduce excessive choice in our lives.

As with noticing, a useful first step is a certain kind of questioning. In this case the questions need to penetrate our inner defences. Of course, they require us first *really to want* to reduce the amount of choice in our lives. We must have realised that too much choice is causing additional stress. (If you are a choice junkie in life's fast lane, then you may as well skip them now and come back to them when your mind is quieter!)

Tool – Finding your tap root

So, once you have acknowledged that the age-old excuse of "I am too busy to take time to think about how I can simplify my life" and have realised that yet another round of "If only …" type statements can be dismissed and sent to the back of your mind, you might want to start asking yourself:

1. What's really important to me in my life at the moment?

2. And again, what's really important to me in my life now?

For most of us the answer to the second of these two questions is a relatively small number of people and items. Now comes the difficult bit. What will you do next? You could consciously spend a weekend purging your home of all its accumulated clutter and then either give it away or sell it via a car-boot sale or eBay. But this may only provide a temporary reprieve! To make reducing the unnecessary choice in your life a regular habit it will help to think specifically about those activities which cause you most stress. If you find shopping stressful because of the proliferation of products, then buy online and make use of the features which many retailers have such as repeat ordering or even clicking on a menu you like, the ingredients of which then, as if by magic, "leap" into your shopping trolley.

A useful metaphor to have in all aspects of your life which involve an excess of choice is a menu with three courses but no choices for any of them!

Synthesising

There is an argument that runs like this: as things are changing so fast it is pointless to go into any great depth in any one area or subject. You'd be better off learning things as and when you need them, "just in time".

There's a certain logic to this point of view. Indeed, evolutionarily speaking, focusing on something in detail on the off chance it might be needed is a waste of discretionary effort and time. In life we need little bits of knowledge from lots of different areas. To take an everyday example, you cook something using a new recipe and, as well as cookery, you need some basic maths and a sprinkling of science.

If you stop to think about it, most of what we do involves synthesising, that is to say combining various individual elements together into a coherent whole. Howard Gardner recently selected the "synthesising mind" as one of his *Five Minds For the Future*. He quotes Bill Clinton's line: "I think intellect is a good thing unless it paralyses your ability to make decisions because you see too much complexity. Presidents need to have what I would call a synthesising intelligence."

Gardner holds back from arguing that we must all just become generalists insisting that we also need to have mastered at least one discipline in detail. Indeed there is a good motivation to study something in depth precisely because it gives pleasure and deep understanding which itself can perhaps be transferred to other contexts.

What perhaps we need more of is the ability to work across disciplines – so scientists and artists can routinely work together, just as those who might term themselves "academic" need to see the value of "practical" work and vice versa. With our increasingly complex identities we need domain-hoppers – those who can take something learned in one place and see some application in another part of their life. A personal example would be the pleasure my wife and I take in life planning, a discipline we have taken from our professional lives (where it might be called strategic planning) and applied it, while undertaking many pleasurable activities at home, to ensure that at least once a year we take time together to take stock of where we are going and reaffirm where we want to be going in the coming year.

In our rapidly evolving world we need to be able to draw information and experiences from many different domains. This is particularly the case in our web-based lives where we need to be able to search widely for trustworthy sources of information and then combine these to provide the answer we are looking for. Computer search engines are brilliant at picking up clues and connecting us to potential sources of help. But the information is presented in its raw and un-synthesised way. If our response is to "cut and paste" our way through our virtual lives, then we are unlikely to thrive.

Unlearning

Once we used pens to write letters and post them, then e-mail came along. Then laptops, mobile telephones and a galaxy of portable hand-held devices arrived, transforming the way we work and communicate. We believed that countries could largely determine their own destiny, then, with the recent financial turmoil, we found out that we are all part of an interconnected monetary system. Dictionaries and encyclopaedias used to be large books annually updated and created by experts. Now, with Wikipedia and the like, they are fashioned and updated in real time by ordinary users throughout the world. Working life today is radically different from working life a decade ago, yet for much of the twentieth century, notwithstanding the invention of the electronic typewriter and fax machine, it was pretty similar for several generations. So much is changing and so fast that although human beings are living longer, it would be easy to become bewildered by it all if you were not able to unlearn.

Too often we talk about the learning curve, when we need to explore the unlearning curve. How quickly and easily can we unlearn things that we have believed for a long while? It's surprisingly tricky. We get set in our ways. The unlearning curve can often be a low flat one unless we actively believe and act in certain ways. We need to be open to new experiences, actively mining them for new ways of doing things. We need time to think things through when we are less hurried. Most importantly we need to be open to feedback from others and willing to act upon it. "Unlearners" regularly ask people to tell them how something went so that they can check that they are doing it differently (and hopefully better) than last time. When things are relatively static we can rely on accepted answers and acknowledged experts. In times of fluidity, it may well be that the situation we are facing is entirely novel, calling on fresh thinking for which there are no established guidelines.

To thrive in today's world we will need to develop a different view of talent. Gone is the reliance on fixed notions of narrow kinds of intelligence like IQ. In the coming years we will be increasingly interested in how the human mind goes about unlearning stuff so that it can constantly expand its intelligence in a range of different contexts. Alvin Toffler's powerful prediction of some forty years ago is demonstrably becoming true: "The illiterate of the 21st century will not be those who cannot read and write, but those who cannot learn, unlearn, and relearn."

Socialising with intent

I have argued that, given that change is changing we may want to adapt our mindware, the mental habits we adopt and tools we use. I now want to suggest that, by the same token, there are certain aspects of our social interaction with others that we may want to do differently.

The idea of social capital, that relationships are the glue which holds society together, has been around for about a century. It was given fresh force in the 1990s by Robert Putnam who defined it as "connections among individuals, social networks and the norms of reciprocity and trustworthiness that arise from them". In other words it is a network, built on trust, of reciprocal relationships. It is the third in a trinity of "capitals" of which the first two are financial (money and belongings) and human (people and talent). No lesser body than the World Bank has adopted social capital as a useful concept: "Social capital refers to the institutions, relationships, and norms that shape the quality and quantity of a society's social interactions ... Social capital is not just the sum of the institutions which underpin a society, it is the glue that holds them together."

In 1990 Robert Putnam argued that, in the US, social capital was declining. He measured this in terms of membership of clubs, participation in voluntary activities, the readership of newspapers, political engagement and so on. Putnam identified the negative aspect of these trends as a kind of inward-looking isolation and individualism which he calls "bowling alone".

Those interested in the idea of social capital have suggested hundreds of ways in which we can build it up, at home and at work. These include such simple actions such as joining a choir, setting up a baby-sitting circle or inviting a friend to go for walk with you, through to more demanding ideas such as becoming a regular volunteer or political activist or setting up some kind of local trading scheme where no money changes hands. All of these kinds of things make good evolutionary and psychological sense. They draw on the reciprocity principle; you scratch my back and I'll scratch yours.

Tool – Speed dating for learning

Originally invented for the purpose of getting a mate, then adapted by entrepreneurs as a means of getting investment from business investors, speed dating is one of the simplest of all means of sharing the learning and experiences of a group.

Each person has to spend no more than one minute with a number of "dates" and you can determine the theme of their conversations (or at least try to!).

Rules:

1. Do it standing up.

2. No double dating! (Keep moving on!)

3. Split the minute evenly. (Listen as well as talk!)

But in today's fast changing world we may need to go beyond social capital thinking. For while any one of the possible actions that you can find if you search the web for "social capital" may be helpful, unless it becomes a systemic pattern of social interaction it may seem like the exception not the rule. A helpful concept in this regard is "collective efficacy". Some thirty years ago Albert Bandura defined self-efficacy in terms of the beliefs a person has in their own capacity to organise and undertake a course of action required to produce what they want. Collective efficacy is the social equivalent of this – a group's shared belief and confidence that it can achieve its desired goal.

Of course, we may need to be wary of the fools' gold of the online versions of collective efficacy such as the instant creation of online interaction via MySpace, Bebo, LinkedIn and the like. The "new best friend" syndrome is immediate but rarely sustaining (just as speed-dating is fine for a warm-up activity but not very nourishing in really building social capital).

Getting under the skin of socialising

In the US two ideas which are illustrative of how we can socialise with intent have caught my attention.

The first exists in one domain and I am going to tweak it a bit and then apply it here. Called "visible thinking", it is the brainchild of Shari Tishman, David Perkins and colleagues at Harvard's Project Zero, a research initiative seeking to help students get better at thinking as they learn. Given that thinking (like learning or, indeed, living) is invisible, Perkins and his team have come up with various ways of making student's thought processes explicit, visible and a real part of the subjects they are studying. Two key questions used by the team are "What's going on here?" and "What do you see that makes you say so?"

These questions tend to be applied by students talking about something they are learning, say a picture, for example. Questions like these are just illustrative. The point is to develop the habit of mind that is constantly exploring the process of thinking. Why did that work? What could I have done differently? Was it helpful to keep going? Was it helpful to take a breather? How did I decide that this was the right answer? Why is this so complicated? What did I do the last time I got stuck? And so on. Questions like these can exist solely in the head of the learner. Or, perhaps more fruitfully still, they can be part of the patterns of social interaction that take place with others.

What if we were to do this in our lives more? Let's call it "visible living". We know that positive self-talk is a powerful tool for dealing with change, but what about audible group-talk? My own experiences and observations of successful groups would suggest that, where people allow themselves to have these kinds of group conversations, groups become much wiser and better able to deal with rapidly evolving situations. A cultural shift takes place in which, through visible living, the quality of reflective and thoughtful interchanges increases. This in turn leads to a cultural shift in the way we go about our learning lives wherever we are. It becomes the goal of any high-performing team to get smarter at sharing its thinking patterns, allowing other members of the group to prevent a seemingly good (but flawed) line of thought to become embedded.

Tool – A "learning with others" routine

What if you automatically went into this kind of routine whenever you got stuck and needed help:

- What's going on here?

- Where have I met this situation before?

- Who do I know who has experienced something like this?

- How can I get their help?

This move from the individual to the group is, in a sense, a result of the web-based landscape in which we live. Once upon a time the written word, first through scribes and later via the printed word, was our main means of sharing our thinking. This was essentially an individual pursuit and, necessarily, fixed in a moment of time. Today thinking out loud on the web has replaced more conventional writing as the mindware of the moment. It is mainly social and very much more fluid in terms of time, with something being thought in Australia, reshaped in China, bounced over to the US and turning up in France in a matter of moments. And the web is a wonderful tool for spotting patterns and trends that might otherwise have remained undetected.

The second example of a new approach is a movement known as "theory of change". It is an attempt to describe and measure what is going on in social change. It started its life in the work of Carol Weiss and colleagues in the US, specifically in evaluating community initiatives, and its influence can now be seen in third and public sector work across the world. It is a very specific kind of systems thinking. The theory of change approach builds on a rich tradition often attributed to Kurt Lewin, seeking to put into practice his famous maxim: "There's nothing so practical as a good theory."

At its core, theory of change approaches seek to lift the lid on how any complex social change works. Why do some things work and other actions fail? In particular it seeks to bring the underlying assumptions about the nature of a social problem, what its solution might be and how a particular action might lead to the solution. It's a way of trying to understand the culture of a group of people.

Theory of change provides helpful scaffolding for collective thinking. Whether it is being applied to a complex issue such as climate change or to a more local challenge such as improving the provision of health care for older people in a particular district, the three stage process works well. I have reduced these to the 3As:

1. *Assumptions* – finding words for underlying hypotheses.

2. *Analysis* – undertaking more detailed analysis to produce possible solutions.

3. *Actions* – moving from mature analysis to implement specific activities.

Tool – The 3As

When you are trying to get to grips with change it sometimes helps to "surface" your underlying theories:

1. Assumptions – "What's going on here?"

2. Analysis – "On what basis do we think this?"

3. Actions – "So what should we do then?"

Using a framework such as the 3As empowers people to talk more openly about why they are doing what they are doing.

While an aspect of the way we connect socially is external, another equally important dimension is (paradoxically, given that "social" normally implies external to self) internal. The phrase currently being used to describe this is "social intuition" – the ability to spot and read cues from those around you very quickly without knowing how you are doing it. To paraphrase Malcolm Gladwell in *Blink* you could think of this as "listening with your eyes". We will be exploring the idea of social intuition in more detail in Rule 3, but at this stage, in a Rule exploring the changing nature of change, it is helpful to understand the evolutionary advantage of social intuition.

In terms of survival, those of our ancestors who could quickly read the intentions of those strangers they met as they hunted for woolly mammoths were more likely to survive and, therefore, to pass on, genetically, the capability for social intuition. Faced with a split second flight or fight decision, this would have been a matter of life or death. Nowadays, as we shall see, it may be a defining characteristic of social expertise.

Rule 1 – The argument so far

The old idea was that change is a gradual process, one that we can adapt to gradually. But this is no longer the case. To thrive today we need different mindware. Specifically, we may want to cultivate the habits of mind associated with imagining, noticing, choosing, synthesising and unlearning. And in terms of our social interactions we may want to learn how to socialise with intent, becoming more expert at surfacing the underlying processes of our engagement with others as we learn and live together.

Last words:

> Minds are of three kinds: one is capable of thinking for itself; another is able to understand the thinking of others; and a third can neither think for itself nor understand the thinking of others. The first is of the highest excellence, the second is excellent, and the third is worthless.
>
> Niccolò Machiavelli

Rule 2 – Real change is internal not external

Everyone thinks of changing the world, but no one thinks of changing himself.

Leo Tolstoy

It's all about us

The whole course of human history may depend on a change of heart in one solitary and even humble individual – for it is in the solitary mind and soul of the individual that the battle between good and evil is waged and ultimately won or lost.

M. Scott Peck

So far we have focused mainly on aspects of evolution that are predominantly technological, scientific, social and so on, as if *they* are the things that matter. But while they certainly form the backdrop to our lives it is the internal landscape that matters more. Now I want to journey into our inner landscape to what's going on inside our hearts and souls.

In some ways we have never "recovered" from the Enlightenment, that exciting period of intellectual development in the eighteenth century when the head was so much in the ascendency, when reason was the primary source for and underpinning of authority. Sure Romanticism partially redressed things, with its emphasis on emotion and imagination, but for most of the subsequent centuries rational thought has been the dominant force. And even now intelligence quotient (IQ), the simple but effective measure of our general cognitive ability, is still there as a reminder of what some people think it really means to be smart. Human beings are so clever that they sometimes forget that cleverness alone is no match for the change which they themselves have unleashed upon the planet. We assume that, whatever the problem, it can be solved provided we can think long and hard when, in reality, life is not as simple as this.

To understand more we need to look more subtly inside ourselves to see how change affects us. Change involves events. A loved one dies. A lack of rainfall forces a family to abandon their homestead. The only shop in a village closes as result of a shift to buying online. Cheques cease to be legal tender as most people rely on credit and debit cards. Each of these situations comes to a head in a moment of time. Yet our reaction to each of these events lasts over a period of days, months or even years. As William Bridges helpfully puts it: "It isn't the changes that do you in, it's the transitions. Transition is a psychological process people go through to come to terms with a new situation. Change is external, transition is internal." And transitions tend to have their own natural rhythms and speeds. In this Rule we will be exploring some of the mindware that is likely to help us manage transitions more effectively.

We have already touched on Kurt Lewin in the Introduction. Let's return for a moment to his three step theory of change; unfreeze–move–refreeze. The first stage inevitably involves a reassessment of the status quo. Take climate change as an example and this might involve an acceptance, albeit a reluctant one, that the actions of human beings do have an impact on the planet and that, therefore, there are things which we might choose to do differently. At such a moment any previous certainties evaporate. The world is suddenly a difficult place to inhabit as it is being governed by a new set of rules. The unfreezing stage can be upsetting and worrying. The second stage tends to be worse, for we are unfamiliar with any of the new rules.

Imagine you were to lose your sight overnight and suddenly had to feel your way around the place, relying on your other senses. It would be very disorientating. Simply finding any kind of equilibrium would involve a major expenditure of effort to avoid bumping into things or not stepping out into the road in front of oncoming cars. Then the third stage

– refreezing – involves establishing new patterns and new ways of doing things. In this case, although slower, using touch and hearing you would hopefully settle on a different way of getting around.

At each of the three stages, Lewin imagines a kind of battle royal being waged around us as we deal with conflicting forces. One is facilitating change. In this example it might be "suggesting" ways in which you can be even more effective in your new circumstances. The other is restraining change, "providing" you with inner voices which only hark back to the days of your full sight.

The common thread in all stressful situations is that they represent a thaw (to use Lewin's ice image) or a change of state. When we are given no option but to do something different, we feel a sense of loss. A familiar situation is being replaced by one which may be difficult or even dangerous.

For change often involves our feelings as much as our thoughts. Mere rationality will not help us to deal with the really difficult transitions we have to face. These tend to be full of emotions, often negative ones to begin with if we do not choose the change. And even if we decide to do something different we may still feel aggrieved that we are doing so. When things are certain and predictable we have relatively easy lives. We follow safe routines and stick to well-trodden pathways. But the minute we are challenged by the uncertain or the new, we have, in a sense, to start again.

Fight or flight?

As human beings evolved, there was good reason why change needed to cause strong feelings. For the sudden disappearance of a source of food or a dramatic change in the weather might have been life-threatening situations. At the neurological level, our minds needed the stimulation of chemicals (such as adrenalin and cortisol) to stimulate us to act. We needed to run from a predator, stand up to an intruder, find the strength in our muscles to go the extra mile to find food. We needed to boost our normal state to survive.

Our stressed responses to change are, in a sense, a legacy of our ability to respond effectively to potentially life-threatening changes to our circumstances. As Abraham Maslow reminded us there is a pecking order of human need. We can only aspire to develop our own potential once our more basic needs – for safety, belonging, esteem and identity – have been met. When we are faced with change we revert to our most basic needs. Which one of us cannot think of times of significant change when we have felt knocked back and found ourselves doing the equivalent of huddling together for warmth with other members of the tribe, such as eating comfort food, wrapping ourselves up in a blanket or watching favourite TV shows which do not challenge us because we know every frame of their unfolding plots?

In most experiences of change, the reactions we have follow a relatively predictable pattern:

And the strength of our feelings tends to depend on two things: the seriousness of the potential impact and the degree to which it was forced upon us rather than chosen.

Of course, change is not as formulaic as this diagram might suggest. It's much messier.

But make no mistake. Change is as much a feature of our inner lives as it is of the great global issues which we were exploring in Rule 1.

The internal consequences of change

Much of the challenge we feel in managing the transitions brought about by change relates to a perception that we are no longer in control. Events seem to be taking over and we may feel powerless to influence them. About fifty years ago psychologist Julian Rotter came up with a theory about the way we view what happens to us. He called it our "locus of control". If you have an internal locus of control, then you believe that you can influence events by what *you* do. If it is external, then you are more likely to account for things by assuming that it is to do with factors *outside* your sphere of influence.

So, for example, if you have an internal locus of control, you might believe that you can get better at doing some aspect of your job if you work at it. But if your focus is external, then you are more likely to assume that any improvements are to do with other factors like a pay rise, a new office or a new boss. People who have an internal locus of control feel motivated from within and more in control of their lives. Human beings have always had to deal with change, but in the white water ride that we are on today we are having to live with more and more uncertainty. Lewin's three stage model implies that change is a separate and bounded phenomenon. But in fact change has become serial such that as fast as one transition settles into its new state, another period of uncertainty opens up.

Interestingly, the more we get our life in control, the happier we are likely to be. Researchers Robert Crosnoe and

Glen Elder have gone a stage further. They have recently shown that "an openness to change in both family life and work life is associated with a 23% greater likelihood of maintaining high levels of life satisfaction". Being open to change is an essential precursor to feeling more in control of events, even if, in reality, these events are controlled by other forces. In Rule 5 we will explore some of the ways in which you can reframe change to your advantage, but meanwhile let's look at some of the mindware that can help us deal with the internal effects of events.

Habits of mind and patterns of action

If we want to become more comfortable with ourselves during change then we may want to cultivate the kind of habits of mind which involve letting go, noticing and naming our emotions, the capacity to rehearse and the development of resilience.

In terms of the way we organise our social interaction there may be an interesting and legitimate tension between our need to be both solitary *and* sociable which we will want to explore.

Letting go

Let's go back to William Bridges for a moment and think more about the psychological process of dealing with a new situation. Why is this so difficult? We have already touched on one of the reasons in the previous Rule, our pattern-making minds. As creatures of habit we get used to something and only give it up reluctantly. Remember how, even after only seeing her for moment you were reluctant to let go of the woman at the window you thought you saw in Rule 1?

The minimum of mental activity can still occasion a certain amount of attachment to an idea. And if we have lived with something – an idea, habit, way of doing something, belief – for a long while, the level of attachment is likely to be much higher. The truth is that letting go is hard even if many self-help books imply that it can be achieved with a small of amount of focused effort. The woman at the window shows how it is not just to do with the rational mind, for we can all too easily see that there is not really anyone there. Neither is it enough simply to rely on the clarity of an alternative idea ("that's the space left by surrounding objects, not a woman").

In terms of managing transitions one of the most important things that we can do, something that will be a recurring feature in the next few pages, is acknowledging that the feelings of change are legitimate and to a certain extent predictable. When it comes to letting go many people mistake the process for the goal. All too easily we can conclude that our way of doing something is *the* one and only way.

Let's suppose that you have always driven a large car and, faced with the increasingly clear evidence of the impact of fossil fuels on global warming, you decide to change your car. It's possible that this will be hard for you. You may not want to let go of your nice big car. It would be easy just to feel grumpy, angry even, about having to change to what you imagine will be a horrid, small, eco-friendly tin on wheels. But you may find it more helpful if you loosen up your mind to the idea that it is often fun to try different ways of doing things. You could investigate top-of-the-range hybrid cars and test drive one. You could look at a number of different smaller cars with a view to finding one that has something you really like about it. In short, you could begin the process of conditioning your mind to be more positive about letting go and remind yourself of other things you have successfully let go (eating quite so much fatty food, being grumpy with your teenage children and so on).

A useful habit to develop when trying to let go of something is to think of it in terms of moving on to something else.

Tool – Moving on

Rather than dwelling on what you are losing start to picture what might be different and better.

Close your eyes. Banish any negative thoughts and spend a few moments in the privacy of your own head thinking about the positive elements of what might happen. What does it look like? How could it help you? How might it be better for you?

Keep making mental space to think about the potential good changes.

Initially this can seem a strange and almost folksy response to difficult stuff happening to you. But once it becomes more habitual it can be a really helpful aspect of your ability to let go.

Noticing and naming emotions

Why are we sometimes so poor at dealing with our emotions? Is it because, in some strange evolutionary way, we worry that displaying them would be a sign of weakness, would give an imaginary enemy some kind of power over us? Or is it that, despite the advent of a more open and less controlled society, we are actually not very good at it?

As children understanding and naming our emotions is one of the most important ways of being a more powerful person. For the act of naming is also an act of taming. Just by recognising what is going on we are gaining some control. Interestingly this approach has recently been corroborated by discoveries in brain science. Brain scanning research has found that naming emotions reduces the intensity of emotional processing in the brain. A group led by psychologist Matthew Lieberman scanned the brains of subjects while they looked at pictures of faces that had different emotional expressions. And where earlier studies have found that naming an emotion seemed to reduce its impact, this one made sure it was actually the naming of the emotion that helped, rather than just naming something else or identifying the emotion in some other way. It turned out that when naming an emotion the activity in part of the brain's prefrontal cortex significantly increased while activity in the amygdala decreased. This did not happen for other tasks.

That change has an important emotional component is an old idea. Look at many medieval cathedrals and you will find a version of the wheel of life. At 12 o'clock is a happy king or queen. But turning clockwise, the same individual becomes distressed as he or she deals with loss and eventually suffering before becoming more hopeful and returning to happier times. The Buddhist mandala is another version of this wheel of life approach and is echoed in a number of world religions. In other words the spiral diagram on page 51 is simply a modern, more psychologically finessed version of what we have known for thousands of years.

By their nature, emotions consume our energies. In the moment it is all too easy not to recognise that they are occurring because we are so involved in them. But, as our self-awareness grows, we can become able to notice emotion as it is occurring. We can stand back from it, look at it from a different perspective, almost as if it were happening to someone else. The very act of noticing emotion helps for it begins to separate us from that emotion and creates space for us to evaluate what's going on for us.

People who routinely notice their emotions get better at picking up their own early warning signs – the pit in the stomach, the clenched fists or the tight shoulders. Sometimes these physical indicators have other observable traits. We start raising our voice or curtly cutting across others when they are speaking (which itself precipitates unhelpful reactions from those around us). They also start to recognise the negative inner voices that assail them at their moments of unhappiness and find ways to "banish" them from their heads.

In terms of dealing with the transitions which are an inevitable aspect of change, if we can routinely notice and name our feelings then we will be better able to see them as part of an overall pattern, one which can and often does get better, as well as being more likely to be able to modify our behaviour in the light of previous experiences.

The capacity to rehearse

Sometimes we need to anticipate rather than simply respond better. Luckily, at some stage in our evolution, human beings realised that they did not actually need to do something to get better at it. We can practise climbing, killing a woolly mammoth, lighting a fire, cooking a meal, riding a bicycle – most things in life – so that when we actually have to do it "for real" we can do it with more aplomb.

Part of this practice involves the acquisition of skills. But a large amount of it is much more about the capacity to imagine what it might be like to do something. It is the second of these attributes on which I want to focus. Back to William Bridges and Kurt Lewin for a moment. Change involves the experience of moving from certainty through uncertainty and then back again to certainty. We leave one job where we know pretty much how things are done and move to another part of the country to another job with a very different set of "rules". At the moment of transition, especially around the time we leave the job, we are likely to feel stressed. What if we were able to imagine the new situation and rehearse in our mind's eye what we will be doing? Would this help?

It turns out that mental rehearsal is indeed an extremely useful habit of mind to nurture. It can increase our performance. (An injured athlete imagines himself running a race from his sofa where he is lying after badly pulling his hamstring and he will derive benefits from this. Those parts of the brain which would normally be ensuring that his legs and arms move together in harmony are stimulated into action as the runner imagines the race or the training.) But, perhaps even more interestingly in terms of dealing with change, the process of mental rehearsal can strengthen us in our ability to change the way we do things and alter our habits.

You only have to look at young children (and many young mammals) to see how many of the early stages of growing up are an elaborate game of "what if?". The child plays at fighting, loving, hunting, parenting, teaching and so on, imagining what it might be like and often copying those around her.

This kind of playful exploration has a value for adults too. The more we can rehearse new situations, whether chosen or imposed, the better we are likely to be able to deal with them. When trying to alter our habitual way of doing something, research into the way we use mental imagery suggests that a particular kind of imagining seems to be helpful. Whereas it may benefit aspiring performers to rehearse their activities "in the first person" (as if they were seeing it with all their senses and really being "in the moment") it seems that this is not the case when you are trying to change the way you do things. In this context it may be more advantageous to imagine yourself from an external or third-person perspective, as others might see you. If you do so you are more likely to see through your intentions.

Developing resilience

Resilience is the ability to bounce back from setbacks. It's the ability to adjust to changes in our daily lives. A major component of resilience is our ability to deal with our feelings, as we have discussed above. But there's more to it than that. For how resilient we are depends to a large extent on our mental "default settings", the degree to which our inner beliefs are strong enough to ensure that we keep the everyday vicissitudes of life in perspective.

Two apparently different aspects of resilience are worth mentioning. The first involves our ability to connect with a higher purpose rather than merely interacting with life on a daily basis – whether this is faith in God, allegiance to a cause or simply an ability to maintain a helicopter view of what happens to you so that you retain the big picture. By doing these kinds of things we are better able to stay focused on a specific direction of travel and things that happen to us are less likely to blow us off course. They are consequently less likely to get us down.

Tool – Building resilience

These aspects of a resilient mindset help and can be practised!

- Expecting change and seeing it as an opportunity for growth.

- Staying fixed on longer-term goals/beliefs.

- Keeping things in perspective.

- Coming up with a number of potential solutions when things go wrong.

- Thinking about what you want rather than worrying about what you fear.

The better we are at practical problem-solving the less likely we are to be blown off track because our computer suddenly crashes, we lose our mobile phone or our car breaks down on the way to an important meeting. People who readily solve problems tend to have cultivated a habit of mind that, whatever the trials and tribulations, leads them to assume that there will be a positive solution. Their problem-solving then becomes a practical indication of their belief that the expenditure of effort is worthwhile. By contrast, those who find it difficult to start trying to solve problems find that they freeze up. They can feel stuck, helpless and increasingly unable to do anything to snap out of the situation in which they find themselves. Their resilience is, unsurprisingly, much lower.

Toggling between social and solitary

At the heart of the social dimension of dealing with the internal turbulence caused by external changes is a paradox: we need to be both sociable and solitary.

In today's world it is easy to be a sociable being. Indeed the Internet has thrived partly because of its ability to bring people together in social networking sites such as Friends Reunited, Facebook, Bebo and so on. And there is no shortage of social gatherings, clubs and interest groups for us to join. In evolutionary terms hanging out with lots of different people is a good idea; we can observe, learn, imitate and consciously not imitate those around us. We can develop more social capital as we discussed earlier because the gene pool for new thinking is bound to be bigger.

The words "networker" and "networking" are relative newcomers to the dictionary in their contemporary sense, to do with actively developing contacts. Having a large and varied network of friends and contacts can be very helpful because, if you also know their specific expertise, you are almost bound to be able to turn to someone in it when you need help on a particular matter.

By the same token a danger of the networked society is that we are so frenetic that we spread ourselves too thin. Our relationships exist only in the sense of being "linked in" to someone else's profile on a networking site or being counted as someone's "friend". We all have belonging needs, as psychologist Abraham Maslow observed more than fifty years ago and, if this level of connection helps to bolster such needs, then they are probably beneficial.

Some years ago in *Power Up Your Mind: Learn Faster Work Smarter* I created the concept of a learning practitioner or LP to which I want to return for a moment. British readers will make the connection between a GP, a general practitioner (or physician), and an LP. What a physician does for our bodies and physical health an LP does for our minds and mental health. Of course, these two worlds are not so distinct and my point in coining the concept was not to suggest that we all need a shrink! It was rather to argue for the importance of the LP role in busy lives. We all need LPs and these are to be found from within our social network. They are the individual members of our friends and family with whom we have a substantial relationship, one that allows us to give voice to our doubts, our half-formed ideas and our hunches without fear of ridicule.

People who cope well with change often have a small number of substantial relationships of the kind I am describing. In fact this kind of support is increasingly referred to as "relationship capital". An aspect of social capital, this phrase seeks to describe the rich mix of friends and associates you can bring to bear on any issue and is something that we will return to in Rule 8. Staying with the financial metaphor for a moment, the network of people around you are assets with real value. But their value is actually released when there is really strong trading between them, in other words when the relationships are mutually beneficial. For knowledge, unlike other finite resources, increases its value once it is shared, enriching the lives of those around us. Unlike money which dwindles as it is disbursed, when a number of people learn a new way of being better able to manage a commonly experienced problem, everyone benefits.

In this context Stephen Covey has a helpful idea. He talks of there being an emotional bank account between people. Like any joint account, we can all make deposits in it (a helpful remark, a useful suggestion, time spent listening to someone's issue) and we can all make withdrawals from it (a request for help, a demanding period where we are only concerned with our own needs, our own self-absorption). But for the marketplace to work the emotional bank account has to seem to be in credit to all of its users. If one person is calling on help from an LP friend of theirs and never reciprocating, then the relationship is unlikely to be sustainable.

Tool – Topping up your emotional bank account

Think of an important relationship in your life.

Think of the way a bank statement has deposits and withdrawals. Now start to think about what a print out of your current emotional bank account would look like.

Each time you have been difficult, grumpy or demanding you have made a withdrawal.

Each time you have been kind, generous or affirming you have made a deposit.

Think back over the last week. How many withdrawals have you made? And how many deposits? Is your account in balance?

From now onwards keep a running tally in your head making sure that you keep your relationship well in credit!

But, helpful as this kind of approach may be, there is another aspect of our lives which we may want to attend to if we are to keep our inner lives well-nourished. This is the deep need that we all have but do not all acknowledge for more solitary moments of quiet. In these moments we can drink deeply from our own inner well of resources. As philosopher Michael Polanyi puts it, "We know much more than we know we know." In the next Rule we will explore one aspect of this – intuition – in more detail.

But for now I simply want to pose some questions. How do you recharge yourself to ensure that you have the inner resilience to bounce back after the trials and tribulations of daily life? Do you enjoy meditation or prayer? Have you even considered trying them? Do you give space for your own daydreams and the quieter thoughts which rise up once you have stopped being busy and "out there"? Are you able to notice when you have become too wrung out with being sociable and need to retreat? Maya Angelou has a lovely sentiment that sums up what I am trying to say: "If one is lucky, a solitary fantasy can totally transform a million realities."

Rule 2 – The argument so far

We have for too long focused our attention on what's changing in the world around us when often the real challenges lie within. While change is undeniably all about us, we may like to dwell more on habits of mind connected with letting go, noticing and naming emotions, mental rehearsal and the development of resilience. And in our social lives this may mean a tension between being sociable and gaining in strength from a network of supportive relationships and being more solitary and careful of the precious resource that is our inner being.

Last words:

> The evolution of the brain not only overshot the needs of prehistoric man, it is the only example of evolution providing a species with an organ which it does not know how to use.
>
> Arthur Koestler

Rule 3 – Slow down

Knowing when to act quickly and knowing when to think and act slowly.

Robert Sternberg, describing intelligent thought

Life in the fast lane

Most of the evils in life arise from a man's being unable to sit still in a room.

Blaire Pascal

There is a sign on the London orbital motorway, the M25, which looks like this.

It informs drivers that they should expect the speed limits to change. Sometimes cars can go at the British national speed limit (seventy miles per hour) while at others they may be reduced to travelling at thirty miles per hour. When you first see this sign you may want to groan inwardly assuming that it is simply the latest affront to your ability to travel at speed. But you need not worry. For far from slowing drivers down these flexible speed limits have actually speeded cars up.

Hold on to the image of a sign that tells you to run at variable speeds, because this is exactly what we are going to explore in this Rule.

Few would dispute that we are all living in the fast lane. Indeed, the response of many people is simply to try to put their foot down harder on the accelerator pedal. You don't need me to tell you that this will just result in burn-out. But I hope I can persuade you of the benefits of going slower sometimes. Here are just a few reasons.

- While we need to be able to respond with speed in certain contexts, our minds actually do much better in response to many of the challenges we face if we slow down. Complex, subtle issues call for a mind which is working in a slower and altogether less conscious way.

- It takes time to become expert in anything.

- When we are at our most creative there is a sense in which time ceases to matter as we are wholly absorbed in the moment of what we are doing.

But before I try to make these points in more detail, let me take a moment more of your time. I started this Rule with the idea of a car but perhaps an aeroplane would have been more apposite. For, a combination of cheap international air travel and mobile communication technology has altered our sense of time as fundamentally as the introduction of the railways and the standardisation of time did in the nineteenth century. The mathematics of travel are easy to compute; we do things in a few hours that used to take us a few weeks. But the curriculum of time involves many other subjects. History changes its meaning. This occurs subtly because, with global travel, the seasons cease to matter, a fact underscored by our ability to eat strawberries, apples and oranges throughout the year. More dramatically, when terrorists flew planes into the twin towers in New York, a defining historical moment, it was visible across the world a few moments later. Geographical distinctiveness is vanishing as global brands turn up in Himalayan villages and Amazonian settlements alike.

Something has also happened to the English language. Two decades ago English was one of several important languages used internationally. But, with the embedding of the Internet, English has become the global lingua franca of communication and commerce. Like all living languages it has always been fluid, but today English is coining new words at a tremendous rate as it attempts to keep up with a changing world.

And of course, all the while, technology drives change in our lives.

These different strands all combine to give us a very different sense of time today. Many people find themselves comparatively rich in terms of money but poor in terms of time. This is an odd twist on our evolutionary tale if you stop to think about it. Once upon a time we lived in tribes as hunter-gatherers. Finding enough food was a daily struggle and at the end of each day we collapsed exhausted into bed. We were time poor and our resources were counted in terms of food in the larder and tools in the cave. Then, after many a while, we learned how to make things in great numbers. Cars, washing machines, irons, refrigerators, radios, televisions and many other useful gadgets rolled off the production lines and we suddenly found that we could do things more quickly. "Couch potato" entered the English language in 1976 to describe the latter day hunter-gatherer with so much time on his hands that he (or she) could idle their time away in front of the television. For a few evolutionary moments it seemed as if we were resource rich *and* time rich. But for most people technology has not bought time. The ubiquitous Blackberry and its equivalents come with us wherever we go, blurring the line between work and leisure for those who cannot turn them off. The result is that today Homo technians frequently lack time.

In the 1930s John Maynard Keynes predicted that "for the first time since his creation man will be faced with his real, permanent problem – how to use his freedom from pressing economic concerns". For several decades this did indeed seem to be the case. Eighty years on and a number of futurologists today reconfigure this challenge to society in terms of high and low skills, suggesting that the latest generation of smart computer technology with its in-built ability to learn and improve will indeed leave those with well-developed skills with time on their hands, while those without will struggle to survive.

A more powerful force than Keynesian economics, however, may well be Parkinsonian experience! Parkinson's Law, you may remember, suggests that work expands to fill the time available. In other words, if technology creates more time for us to use, then we will simply take longer doing the other things we need to do in the time we have available. Interestingly, psychologists have demonstrated the truth behind Parkinson's Law with a simple experiment involving the solving of anagrams. Subjects were all given three different lengths of time – five, ten and twenty minutes – to solve their puzzles and researchers found that, the more anagrams people were given, the more they solved and vice versa. Perhaps more pertinently, those who started off thinking that they only had five minutes kept up their higher work rate even when they were given longer amounts of time. In other words, we seem to be very good at adapting our work rate to the time available! Mindset matters and, as we will discover later in this Rule, certain habits of mind can be more conducive than others in navigating our way through life.

One more thing. The semantics of slow and fast living are frequently not favourable to advocates of slow living. To be a slow learner at school is another way of saying that we are dim-witted. It is also associated with a lack of energy and an unwillingness to act. Even the proverbial "slow and steady wins the race" hardly makes being slow sound attractive.

It seems likely that quite different attitudes to time have become associated with those born at different times. We have even invented the idea of Generation X (those born in the 1960s and 1970s) and Generation Y (those born in the 1980s and 1990s) to describe these and other fundamentally different world views. A number of recent surveys have made clear that Generation Y-ers are impatient. They see rapid change as inevitable and this is nowhere clearer than in their attitude to employment; Generation Y-ers love the idea that they will constantly be on the move and are likely to have greater loyalty to a favourite brand than to an employer. Generation Y-ers tend to want more flexibility in their lives, trading lower salaries for the ability to spend time doing the things they enjoy. In this sense they are better at slowing down than their Generation X parents.

Slow wins the race

In his groundbreaking book *Hare Brain, Tortoise Mind: Why Intelligence Increases When You Think Less*, psychologist Guy Claxton made a compelling case for the tortoise more than a decade ago. He argues that there are three different speeds of thought. The first is the instinctive survival mode such as when we have to take sudden evasive action in a car. We do it instantly and only later on work out what we did. The second speed, the one we use most of the time, is the one we use when we are consciously thinking things through. Shall I go shopping today or can we manage with what we have in the larder? And the third tortoise mind – more dreamy and less purposeful than the other two – is the slowest of the three.

It is this last of the three which Claxton suggests is the underused resource. Drawing on a range of scientific evidence he shows how certain states of mind are better able to make sense of more complex issues which cannot easily be conceptualised. Most of us can think of times when we have had a dull sense of unease about a decision we have made. By any standard of hard logic or standard speed thinking we can rationalise why we are doing whatever it is. But the nagging doubts will not go away. Often the questions which will help us to resolve our worries have not yet even surfaced. They still remain to be formed. To help them surface we need consciously to slow our thought processes, putting our minds into the kind of receptive state in which the kinds of questions we need to ask ourselves will bubble up. Only once we have almost slowed our minds to tortoise speed is it likely that we will find the questions (and then the answers) which have so far eluded us.

The kinds of tough issues facing all of us – climate change, equitable sharing of global resources, new technology and the others mentioned in Rule 1 – will not all respond to either of the first speeds at which we think. They also need the "slower ways of knowing" advocated by Claxton (and developed further by both of us in *The Creative Thinking Plan*).

If you don't believe us, take a moment to look at this list:

- A sense of not meeting goals

- Difficulty in getting organised

- Difficulty in getting started

- Too many projects going on at the same time and not being properly seen through

- A restless search for excitement

- Low tolerance for boredom

- Easy distractibility

- A tendency to drift in and out of conversations or reading resulting in confusion.

Do you recognise any of these symptoms in your life? I have adapted them from *Driven to Distraction* by psychiatrists Edward Hallowell and John Ratey. If children exhibited such symptoms they would probably be diagnosed as having ADD (attention deficit disorder), also known as ADHD where the extra H stands for hyperactivity. These are the kinds of things that happen when our brains only operate in fast mode. We become dissatisfied dilettantes, flitting from one item to the next and never really engaging with one in any detail, either in normal thinking speed or in the slower more reflective state I am focusing on.

Perhaps we are reaching some kind of tipping point in the evolution of the human brain with so much stimulation on offer from technology. Just as our brains expanded to cope with our ability to use language and organise our lives for communal living some 200,000 years ago, so now they might be evolving and adapting as a consequence of the technology on which many of us depend. Maybe we will find shortly that we *can* achieve the quality of thought we need while multitasking as our minds adapt to the new circumstances in which we live.

Generation Y-ers, for example, will routinely be on a laptop playing a game and messaging their friends, while watching the television, flicking through a book and idly checking text messages as they come in on their mobile phone. (The words I am using here to describe what these different devices do may of course be out of date by the time you read this, but you will hopefully recognise what I am saying.)

But just how far can our attention be divided before we are so far in deficit that we cease to function properly? Is Homo sapiens becoming pathologically unable to concentrate for more than a few moments? Whether or not you are persuaded by the earlier tortoise argument, you may at least concede that it is unlikely that the complex and very real challenges facing us are unlikely to be solved just with stop-start bursts of thinking. Divided attention has, I want to argue, become a habit of mind for many people. And while it may be helpful in some situations – preparing supper for friends, for example, where we may want to move between table-laying, flower-arranging, ingredient assembling, food preparing and getting clothes ready – when more sustained concentration is required or when the problem is a troublesome one which has not yet formed clearly enough in our heads, we may be better off being in the moment rather than flitting from one thing to the next.

In Rule 2 I talked about the flight or flight response, our inbuilt survival mechanism that enables us to run fast, climb quickly or battle against an intruder. Think of any time when you have had to summon up extra energy under great pressure and you will understand why no one would want to make a decision in this state unless they were forced to. It's helpful only for the life or death situations for which it evolved – indeed, at the neurobiological level it appears that parts of our brain are temporarily "switched off" to enable us to use all our available energy to survive. The slower state of mind is the one that has evolved to enable our minds to grapple with the more complex issues of life we face today.

As William Collins reminds us: "It's that willingness to slow down and examine the mysterious bits of fluff in our lives that is the poet's interest." A reduction in speed has always been of interest for writers; now we can all do more of what poets do.

It takes time

There is of course another fundamental reason why we need to recalibrate our attitude to time and that is simply that acquiring expertise takes time. It's easy to forget that, although we can travel to far-flung parts of the world in a few hours, becoming really good at something requires many years of practice. In fact, according to one of world's leading researchers on this topic, Anders Ericsson, it typically takes about ten years. Whether you are a concert violinist or a star footballer it is likely that you will have clocked up thousands of hours of intensely disciplined, often solitary practice. Interestingly one of the reasons that performers seem able to spend such a long time practising is that they are constantly striving to better their previous performance and achieve more control. And control is achieved, paradoxically, when the performer, precisely because they have practised so diligently and consciously, stops having to think about what they are doing but can allow their creative self to take over. At this moment they have achieved an altogether different state of mind.

There is another good reason why being immersed in a task is a good idea; it is simply more efficient. Generation Y, as we saw earlier, favours a multitasking approach to life, flipping between hand-held device, conversation and other flat screens. But research into multitasking is clear: we do not learn or perform as well as we could when we are distracted. As UCLA's Professor Russell Poldrack puts it: "Multi-tasking adversely affects how you learn. Even if you learn while multi-tasking, that learning is less flexible and more specialised, so you cannot retrieve the information as easily. …The best thing you can do to improve your memory is to pay attention to the things you want to remember. … When distractions force you to pay less attention to what you are doing, you don't learn as well as if you had paid full attention."

If you want to get better at complex calculations or prepare a difficult speech or drive safely, you are better off not trying to read the newspaper, shop online or use your mobile phone at the same time.

Even if you are not an expert performer yourself you will probably have experienced this curious effect by which, over time, something that you work at consciously becomes an automatic response. Driving a car is often cited as an example which most of us will have experienced. In a model often attributed to W. C. Howell, we can think of acquiring a skill like this as follows:

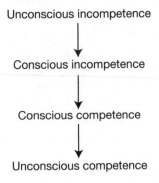

Unconscious incompetence

↓

Conscious incompetence

↓

Conscious competence

↓

Unconscious competence

Most of us will remember the stage of our learning when we needed total concentration. A question from a passenger could throw us off the careful sequencing of using mirrors, signalling, anticipating and all the motor skills we needed to translate these into safe control of the car. Then one fine day, some while after we had passed our driving test, we realise that we can actually talk about the meaning of life while at the same time driving in automatic mode. It is a wonderful moment!

Expert performers manage to stay for longer at the conscious competence stage, deliberately working out what distinguishes an excellent from a good enough performance. Most of us can't wait to get to the stage when we can stop being consciously aware of what we are doing and just get on and do it well enough. Driving a car safely is something that takes considerable practice for most of us to learn to do. Becoming an elite athlete or a great chef or Formula One racing driver takes many hours of deliberate practice. Although skilled performers can do what they do *without* thinking, they also know that they need to practise the hard parts repeatedly, in many different ways and in different contexts, until the level of the performance is better still.

In the examples above I have focused on expertise. But there is a higher aspect of human evolution which both in different ways aspire to, our individual creativity. As we have already seen, when Abraham Maslow suggested that human needs are hierarchical, starting with such basic elements as having food in their bellies and a roof over their heads and ending with the idea of self-actualisation, he was also restating a belief in the higher potential and creativity of the species. We exist not to eat or sleep but to realise our inner potential.

There are obvious evolutionary parallels to Maslow's psychology. We had to hunt for our food, find a dry place to shelter and some congenial tribe members to share it with before it was sensible to expend our energies painting stories on the walls of a cave. Interestingly something strange happens to our sense of time when we are at our most creative. It is what Mihalyi Csikszentmihalyi calls "the state of flow". This is when we are totally absorbed in a creative task – writing, making music, building a complicated Lego model, playing chess, undertaking a difficult climb – when time ceases to matter as we are wholly absorbed in the moment of what we are doing. We are concentrating so much on what we are doing that although alive to every little bit of feedback from any move we might make, say putting our foot on a small ledge, we are utterly unaware of what's going on around us. We are in a mental state where distractions do not exist. Hours go by but we may only experience them as a few moments. We are enjoying what we do for its own sake, not because it is going to achieve any specific benefit to us or to others.

At one level in terms of our evolution, this could be seen as wasteful. Great chunks of discretionary time – the hours we choose to spend on things which we do not have to do – are wasted; no one is better fed, more warmly clothed or living in a better protected home. All that has been achieved is a greater sense of happiness in an individual.

But this would be a very short-sighted assessment of the flow state. For it is in such moments that great invention and creativity have been found. Discoveries made which undoubtedly advance the human cause. Indeed, far from deriding flow we should treasure it, finding ways of cultivating its absorption. For it is in such moments that we may yet be able to solve the more complex issues which we face. On this basis it should be the job of every primary school in the world to teach children how to cultivate the state of flow! The new ideas that might flow from this are the memes we met in Rule 1. As with biological evolution, not all of them will improve our chances of survival. But some of them will.

If nothing else the nurturing of the state of flow would release a certain kind of energy into the world. For it is this force that Csikszentmihalyi sees as being behind our ability to generate high levels of attention and so enables us to concentrate for long periods of time. Such energy would be the perfect counterpoint to the kinds of ADD symptoms listed on page 71. And unlike the kind of energy we need, for example, to sprint for a hundred metres, creative energy is sustainable, refuelling itself through the act of creation.

Habits of mind and patterns of action

If we want to slow down and so become more effective during change then we may want to cultivate the kind of habits of mind which involve being, deferring, getting better at surfacing issues and reflecting.

In terms of our social patterns of action, it may be that there is an interesting and legitimate tension between our need to be both solitary *and* sociable which we will want to explore.

Being

To be or not to be was the iconic question with which Hamlet pondered whether he should remain alive or not. But for many people today it can be rephrased to describe the tension between doing or being. As our busy lives get busier most of us are more human doings and less human beings.

We have even coined an embarrassing phrase "quality time" to mitigate our inability to slow down. Quality time is what we do when, often through clenched teeth, it becomes obvious that we have got the speed of our lives out of kilter. Busy working parents "timetable" it, unaware that the recipients of it – often their children – might not want a sudden intrusion of full-on parental presence. Busy executives schedule it so that their reluctant juniors can have short bursts of their attention.

Some would urge us all to revert to a different time, radically rethinking our lives and reverting to an earlier, technology-free era. But I do not think that this is necessarily desirable and I am sure it is hopelessly unrealistic. It does not actually take much to rebalance your life. If you have ever bought a new tyre for your car you will have noticed that once it is fixed to the chassis it has to be spun and then "rebalanced". If it does not spin true, then the fitter will clip a small piece of metal to one side of the rim of the wheel to ensure that it is in balance. A wheel that is not so treated will start to wobble and could eventually lead your car to lurch off the road and become unsteerable.

It is similar for us. If we do not take small steps to rebalance our lives we can all too easily spin out of control. In the context of this Rule – the desirability of sometimes running at a slower speed – we need to find the equivalent of the small pieces of metal which will help us to run smoothly. An obvious pressure point, the tension between home and work life – sometimes referred to as the work–life balance – has been much written about. There are a range of practical things that we can do to protect our home time and I do not intend to add to the list. Most of these approaches operate on a kind of deficit model, where work is seen as the evil taking us away from our family pleasures and causing us stress.

Carl Honoré has done much to promote what is increasingly being referred to as the Slow Movement, a growing realisation that we cannot simply carry on getting faster. The law of diminishing returns is beginning to apply. He quips that you can even do courses in speed yoga or speed meditation these days, and admits to a momentary thought that it would be a good idea to write a book of one-minute bedtime stories to read to your child, before dismissing this as a ridiculous thought! For, when reading to anyone a significant element of what is valuable is the process of spending time enough to become immersed in the experience.

The Slow Food movement, originally founded as part of a protest against the impact of fast food outlets like McDonalds in Rome but now part of a much broader global movement, is another example of rebalancing our attitude towards food. Its aims are to "counteract fast food and fast life, the disappearance of local food traditions and people's dwindling interest in the food they eat, where it comes from, how it tastes and how our food choices affect the rest of the world". But it would be easy to take out the word "food" and substitute the word "life" to establish an organisation which could really promote the benefits of the tortoise approach.

I am interested in some of the small steps we can take to cultivate the kind of changed mental state that will enable us to be more and do less. The first step is to see the value of slow. The second step is to find the small changes we can make that will have most leverage. I have two contenders for influence: one that feeds the body and one the soul. For some of us simply to take time to do that most primitive and bonding of all human activities, taking time to prepare, cook and eat a meal together once a day, is all that it takes.

So many good things flow from a simple rebalancing of our lives. And if you want food for the soul, then finding some activity where on a regular basis, ideally daily, you can lose yourself in something where you are no longer consciously straining at the leash of life may well be the answer. This might be achieved simply by taking a walk in landscape conducive to you, by lying for longer than is necessary in a hot bath, by making music, by doing some yoga, by gardening or by expending enough time playing with your child that you truly empathise with her imagined world. Often, as we found when thinking about the state of flow and the acquisition of expertise, we may only achieve a "spiritual" release via conscious effort and practical activity. If you cavil at my use of the word spiritual in these contexts, some of which may seem too mundane to you, then either try it for yourself or adopt more "conventional" spiritual pastimes such as prayer or meditation!

How we choose to slow down is a matter of personal choice. Whether we choose to is, I am arguing, not a real option if we do not want our lives to spin out of control. How we view the way we spend our lives really does matter. Psychologist Ellen Langer reminds us of this by presenting the results of a really telling experiment. Volunteers were given Gary Larson's *Far Side* cartoons to sort into categories. One group is told that they are embarking on a job of work. The other is encouraged to think of the activity as play. Guess which group enjoyed it more and did it better? The playful one, of course. Indeed there seems to be an interesting link between having the confidence just to slow down and "be" and being able to be playful as adults.

Indeed "being" is very close to the idea of mindfulness, also developed by Langer. Blending Eastern philosophy and psychology, Langer has identified three elements of mindfulness. It involves:

1. Continuously creating new categories (not stuck in the groove of thinking that there is a "woman at the window").

2. An implicit awareness of other perspectives and, perhaps, most importantly for understanding the idea of "being".

3. An openness to new information.

It is a playful, naive openness to the experience in which you find yourself that seems to be a key element of being in the moment.

Tool – Letting the phone ring in your life

How often do you rush to answer the phone or other electronic device immediately? Even during meals? When you are out on a walk with friends or family? Do you really want to do this?

Just set phones and other devices to "silent" or "off" regularly and enjoy the opportunities for "being"!

Deferring

Sometimes put off until tomorrow what you can do today! Procrastination is the friend of time! Put off gathering the rosebuds while ye may! Perhaps such homespun heuristics are the products of an age where a society dependent on daylight hours for necessary tasks had to portray procrastination as a form of laziness. One of the flaws of the categorising human mind is its tendency to prefer binary alternatives. Not doing something instantly becomes wasting time. The only way to keep up is to work faster. And so on. There is a fashionable view that, simply by going away you are storing up more work and anxiety for yourself. For while you may be enjoying yourself, your in-box will be filling up with e-mails. And the minute you return, the contents of the in-box must be dealt with. The received wisdom from this kind of world view all too easily becomes "I'm simply too busy and slowing down is bound to make things worse." All too easily we can stop noticing the fact that we are simply working longer and harder to stand still.

There must be another way! As Albert Einstein memorably reminds us, a useful definition of insanity is "doing the same thing over and over again and expecting different results". What if we could train our minds to default to another setting where not doing something but deciding to, as it were, "sleep on it" was seen as a smart thing to do? What if always jumping into action was to become a dumb thing to do?

Stephen Covey has a neat idea which he calls the "pause button". Using the pause button on the video or DVD remote control as a metaphor for freezing the action, he imagines successful people as being able to stop themselves between something happening and our reactions to what has happened. If you like this is an aspect of what many people might think of as emotional intelligence. I'd like to extend and adapt this idea to deal with our deeply embedded habit of immediately jumping into action. If we could all press an imaginary button that helps us to ask "Do I really need to do this now or might it be better if I returned to it when I am in a more relaxed frame of mind?" then we might find it easier to slow down.

Tool – Pressing your pause button

Next time you feel yourself about to leap into action press your own pause button.

Close your eyes and count to ten.

Ask yourself whether you really need to act now or whether it can wait until later.

Who knows. Later you may decide that it was not so important after all …

Specifically we might decide consciously to put off some of the things which we would otherwise have tried to cram into an already busy day, to get better at deferring. A friend of mine has a really helpful way of "deferring" people's e-mail requests while he is either on leave or choosing to give his mind a break. His auto-response reads something like this: "Sorry, but I will not be answering my e-mails until <date> and will not even be reading any e-mail sent to me before this date. However if your e-mail is really important, then please resend it on <date> and I will, of course read it then." Many of us assume, quite wrongly, that simply sending an e-mail is an act of communication which confers an obligation on the recipient to respond. At a stroke this auto-response turns the table on this conventional assumption. Needless to say my friend ends up dealing with a small number of wanted e-mails on his return where others are grimly ploughing their way through hundreds feeling their stress levels rising!

In the language of finance we use the verb "defer" to describe legitimate activity to ensure that we are not liable for tax unnecessarily in any one financial year. Similarly in education, students going to university can, in many cases very wisely, defer their entry, creating a gap year between school or college and university. There is a famous experiment commonly referred to as the "marshmallow test" developed by Professor Walter Mischel at Stanford University. Four-year-olds are given a marshmallow and told that they can either eat it immediately or wait. If they wait they are offered more marshmallows. The experiment divides children into grabbers and deferrers. Now that the original 4-year-olds are growing up it is possible to see that there is a strong correlation between those who are able to defer their gratification and success in life, specifically in terms of social competence, assertiveness and academic results.

Deferring, as you can see, has some proven benefits in this very specific example. But I am also arguing that deferring has other benefits, for, as with the example of the e-mail auto-response, the act of the deferring may mean that you defer it forever! By slowing your response down you may end up never responding. The moment passes. What seems important turns out not to be and life moves on with a slower but deeper rhythm.

Surfacing

Do you recognise this experience: moving from one room to another in your home you find yourself wondering what you have come in to get or do? Worrying that your mind is cracking up, you start desperately trying to remember what it is you came in for. Your mind remains a blank and you sheepishly return to the room you just left. As you get back to where you started, something pops into your mind. It was a pair of scissors you needed. Mysteriously, something in your memory is triggered by your return to the place where you first had the scissor thought.

Or you are chatting away to a friend and on the point of telling her something interesting. Perhaps you are recommending a book or recalling the name of a mutual acquaintance. Suddenly your mind goes blank. The harder you try to remember the worse it gets. So you stop trying to recall whatever it was and, almost magically, into your brain pops the thing you had forgotten.

These sorts of things happen to most of us, probably with greater frequency as we get older! They illustrate how effectively our minds work when we stop thinking too hard! For in both examples once our mind is able to operate in a softer, slower, less focused way, it does a good job for us.

This kind of softer seeing of the world is a habit of mind that can be cultivated. It is particularly helpful when we are grappling with questions or issues which are not yet clearly enough formed in our heads to be scrutinised more energetically. Some people find that the act of relaxing their eyes so that vision becomes blurred or even closing them is a good cue to the mind to calm down. In such a state we often find it easier to allow shapes and patterns to emerge.

Often it is the more complex or ambiguous issues in our life which are the least well formed. All we have to go on is a sense of unease, of unfulfilled potential or perhaps of anxiety. If we can bring an issue to the surface of our mind we are more likely to be able to explore it. And the slower mind is good at surfacing things. Try this technique developed by Guy Claxton and myself and adapted from *The Creative Thinking Plan: How to Generate Ideas and Solve Problems in Your Work and Life.*

Tool: Soft focus seeing

Try adapting this exercise.

Relax the focus of your eyes and take in the whole scene at once. Whatever you are doing, defocus your gaze and see all the movement at once! Be aware of what is going on in the periphery of your vision as well as what is happening at the centre. See the "big screen".

If it's raining, look at a rain-spattered window. Track the movement of one raindrop as it makes its way down the pane. Watch it very carefully. Now shift focus and be aware of the whole window. See all the movement at once.

Or you could lie on your back and do the same thing with the clouds. First watch one little bit; then be aware of the whole motion.

Bring your two hands up so that they are about a foot out from each ear. Extend the index finger of your right hand and waggle it gently. Look straight ahead, and see if you can detect the movement of the finger. Move your right hand backwards and forwards till you have found the point where you are just able to sense the movement. Be aware of your attention being drawn to the periphery of your field of vision. Now do the same thing with the left hand. Waggle both fingers at once. Be aware of them both simultaneously.

Notice whether you have been totally oblivious of what is in front of you, bang in the middle of your field of vision. See if you can include that into your simultaneous picture. Stop waggling the fingers. See where you have to put them to be aware of their presence when they are not moving. Is it different?

Reflecting

Insights often come to us when we are in the slower mode that has been the focus of this Rule. Famously Archimedes had his "a-ha!" moment while in his bath once he had started relaxing after many hours of hard work in his workshop. Apocryphally many people notice how their best reflective thoughts occur to them when they have switched off, if not in the bath or shower, then while jogging or snoozing or daydreaming.

Once we have become more adept at running at variable speeds then we can begin to anticipate such moments as these when we can – catch our mind unawares, as it were. The more we can harvest these reflective insights the better. For such reflections often allow us to crystallise our thinking about issues. Traditionally, in an age of diary keeping and letter writing, an obvious way of creating time to reflect would have been to set aside a few minutes, perhaps on a daily basis, to extract the meaning from a day's experience in one or other of these forms. For most people e-mail is a much more instrumental medium and is more likely to involve exchanges of information about practical arrangements rather than more reflective thinking. Text messaging is the same, although this more recent form of communication with its "How r u?" and "Hows it goin?" potentially can be used to invite, albeit terse, moments of reflection.

But in blogging there is a really interesting new and rich vein of reflective activity. Originally conceived as logs or diaries (weblogs), blogs are now used by many as a means of personal promotion. But for some it is clearly a useful form of measured reflection, widely shared into the blogosphere. Evolutionarily speaking this is a potentially useful (and distracting) source of learning for the species!

Social intuition

In Rule 1 I introduced you to the idea of speed dating, the process used both for the purposes of meeting lots of potential "mates" but also, increasingly, for sharing knowledge quickly in a business networking context. Clearly speed dating would not be an appropriate pattern of social interaction in a Rule devoted to slower ways of being!

Instead let's think of what slow dating might look like. Imagine a process where, simply by being with others you could learn from them. Researchers like David Myers have described this as "social intuition". It is quite possible to construct a good evolutionary case for its power: successful survivors would have had the ability to read complex social situations intuitively and so work out whether a new situation involved danger or not by unconsciously picking up clues from the social context. But this form of social intelligence is not just about survival. In its more developed social form, if we can get better at heeding the promptings of our social intuition alongside our more conscious thought processes, we will have access to much richer data about what is going on around us.

Social intuition has a number of elements. At its simplest it includes merely being exposed to other people. So, for example, just spending time with people who, for example, use certain ways of greeting each other, say a good wholesome hug as opposed to a tentative handshake, will rub off on us. In the context of deliberately seeking to cultivate our ability to slow down, then one really simple choice we can make is to avoid the worst excesses of our very adrenalin-driven society by choosing to spend time with people who relish slower ways of knowing and being.

Then there is the much stronger component, sometimes referred to as emotional contagion – the phenomenon that means that our emotions are affected by the emotions of those around us. If an actor reads an emotionally neutral speech in different voice inflections, one happy, one neutral and one sad, then listeners will tend to align their view of the content of the speech according to the inflection of the actor's voice. Interestingly, on the basis of just listening to the different versions of a speech like this, listeners consistently "disliked" the creator of the sad version more than the other two! We will return to this and other aspects of social intuition in Rule 9.

But there is an interesting paradox at the heart of the idea of social intuition. For while it seems increasingly clear that we can access our intuition better if we are prepared to cultivate a calmer and more receptive mindset, the process of social intuition can be remarkably rapid. This is sometimes referred to as "thin slicing". In other words we can form judgements about other people based on only a few seconds worth or a very thin slice of information. It is easy to see why: as he moved around the savannah, early man had to sort out quickly friend from foe even before any conscious exchanges had taken place. It turns out that we are actually rather good at making split-second judgements. Nevertheless we can also "read" a situation quite wrongly.

In terms of desirable patterns of social interaction then, it seems reasonable to conclude that we may want to invest more time and energy in heeding the full range of messages we pick up from being with other people. Some of these intuitions arrive unbidden; some are the result of more measured analysis. Neither is necessarily right or reliable. But taken together they provide a richer way of seeing the world.

Rule 3 – The argument so far

We have for too long assumed that as the world speeds up, so should we. Instead we may find it more helpful to adopt a different approach to time, learning when the ability to slow down is likely to be more fruitful, enabling us to tap into our deeper, more profound selves. Habits of mind connected with being, deferring, surfacing and reflecting may be of particular interest to us. And we may wish to learn how to be more socially intuitive.

Last words:

> The hare brain has had a good run for its money. Now it's time to give the tortoise mind its due.

> Guy Claxton

Rule 4 – We can all change the way we see the world

To improve is to change; to be perfect is to change often.

Winston Churchill

Pioneers and stay-at-homes

The vast majority of human beings dislike and even actually dread all notions with which they are not familiar ... Hence it comes about that at their first appearance innovators have generally been persecuted, and always derided as fools and madmen.

Aldous Huxley

When many of us stayed at home, too worried about long and possibly dangerous journeys, others left the safety of the log fire for the unexplored expanses of new worlds. Some of us craved the risk of the new – we loved the unexplored, we enjoyed bringing our own preferences and character to bear on virgin soil. Others of us preferred certainty, safety and a familiar environment.

Few would dispute this description of the great ages of exploration in the third quarter of the last millennium. But is it true today? Are only some people capable of being pioneers? Are some set to be stay-at-homes? It is certainly the prevailing wisdom that only some people are temperamentally suited to dealing with the kind of risk and change associated with pioneering.

One of the most widely used descriptions of the way we respond to new ideas is the change curve proposed by Everett Rogers in *Diffusion of Innovations* in 1962. Rogers was primarily speculating about the way human beings respond to technological innovation, but his model is used much more broadly than this. Essentially he argues that only a small proportion of us, 2.5 per cent, are pioneers (or innovators) and that only 16 per cent, the innovators and early adopters, are likely to take any significant risk (by using something until it has been widely accepted by others).

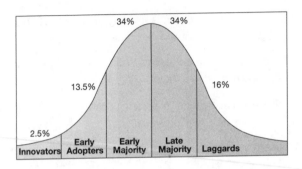

Personally I have always found Rogers's description of my fellow human beings far too neat, an inevitable result of using the bell-curve model. It also seems to be based on some deeply pernicious early nineteenth century ideas about fixity of ability. But I like the idea of early adopters and find it a useful way of imagining reactions to change. And in this Rule I want to argue that, notwithstanding some important personality preferences we may have, it is possible for us all to be much more pioneering in our attitude to change. Indeed I will go further by suggesting that, given that rapid change is here to stay, there is, in a sense, no home fire by whose warmth we can metaphorically stay, leaving the dangerous job of exploration to a pioneering few.

For many of us today the change curve looks more like this:

While I disagree with the neatness and inevitability of the Rogers approach, his analysis of the process by which people change their minds seems really helpful. He suggests that this has five stages:

1. Knowledge – we become aware of an innovation and have some idea of how it works.

2. Persuasion – we form a favourable or unfavourable attitude towards it.

3. Decision – we engage in activities that lead to a choice to adopt or reject the innovation.

4. Implementation – we put an innovation into use in our own life.

5. Confirmation – we evaluate the results of our decision to innovate.

Think of the way you have started using a new piece of technology, a new medicine, a new process or a new way of doing something and run through these five stages to see if they work for you. But still it is easy to feel that the messiness of life is being somehow too much neatened up when you look at approaches like the one Rogers proposes.

By contrast Malcolm Gladwell offers a different image for the way ideas spread and people change. He uses the image of the tipping point.

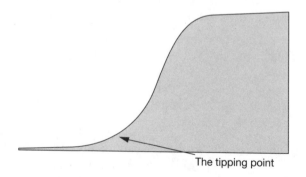

The tipping point

Gladwell's metaphor is taken from the way that viruses spread. Think of an outbreak of flu, for example. For many days a small number of people snuffle away, then suddenly you hear on the news that part of your local hospital is closed because of an outbreak of influenza which means that there are not enough nurses to care for patients. Citing various examples – the proliferation of crime in New York and the way *Sesame Street* developed into a television success are just two instances – he concludes that there are three characteristics to the way ideas become epidemics and take off:

1. They are contagious. Like flu you "catch" them.

2. Small causes often have large effects.

3. Change happens suddenly.

The last of these three characteristics is probably most important. Think back to the pond in Rule 1: one moment the weed was virtually unnoticeable, the next it covered the entire surface of the pond.

Gladwell concludes that change today can be driven by comparatively few people. A good example of this might be the way that blogging took off. The context in which change occurs is also highly significant. Small adaptations can have large impacts. He uses the example of how crime on the New York subway system was significantly reduced by a zero tolerance attitudes towards graffiti. The idea of a tipping point is in many ways more of our time than the Rogers curve with its suggestion of orderly innovation.

The white water of change

For many of us today it seems as if we are on a rollercoaster. We are flying down a river with no time to stop and think. While we may hear ourselves thinking that things will settle down once we have got through whatever new aspect of change we are dealing with, we know really that this will not happen. For change today is endemic. It is here to stay with all the force of an epidemic. We can't alter this fact. But we can change the way we see the world.

As management guru Tom Peters puts it: "Winners must learn to relish change with the same enthusiasm and energy that we have resisted it in the past." To get on we need to cultivate an openness to change.

This begs an important question. Are certain personality types more predisposed to change than others? In other words, will what Tom Peters is exhorting us to do be easy for some and harder for others? As I write Barack Obama is well into his term of office. His successful presidential campaign was run with Obama's constant assertion that he was ready for change. This gave a very clear message to voters about the degree to which Obama is outward-looking, questioning the status quo and potentially creative.

For some time there has been consensus about the main dimensions of personality. Sometimes referred to as the Big Five, these include extraversion, agreeableness, conscientiousness, neuroticism and openness to experience. These five areas of personality were derived from statistical analysis and are not linked to any one particular theoretical perspective. Of the five, openness to experience is clearly relevant to our thinking here. Openness (as opposed to closed-mindedness) describes the complexity of an individual's inner life. It is relatively evenly distributed across the population. In other words there are roughly as many people who are open to change as there are those who are closed to it. Openness to experience involves our imagination, our aesthetic sensitivity, our attentiveness to inner feelings, our preference for variety and our intellectual curiosity.

Our openness to experience generally declines with age according to this specific measure. Indeed the stereotypical "grumpy old man" tag is an indication of how, in the perception of society, people get more set in their ways as they grow older. The real question is whether or not it is possible to learn to become *more* open to change or not. And on this issue a number of modern psychologists and educators are clear that we can indeed become more open to change; we can learn to be more receptive to it by adopting some of the habits of mind I will suggest later on in this Rule.

The glass half full

The person credited as the founder of positive psychology is Martin Seligman. In *Learned Optimism: How to Change Your Mind and Your Life*, he deals head-on with the old view that how we see the world is simply a matter of inherited characteristics or a product of our environment. Seligman shows the value of being positive, how it improves health and mood and how it can transform our ability to persist rather than giving up in the face of difficult events.

Tool: The half full or half empty test

If you are not sure how positive you are, try this simple test:

Record the likelihood of this happening to you within the next year: 10 = it is bound to, 1 = It is bound not to

1. Someone tells you how much they like you.

2. You are praised for having a good idea.

3. Someone compliments you on how attractive you look.

4. You get a promotion at work.

5. You win something.

6. You meet someone special.

7. You really enjoy your next vacation.

8. You make a meal which everyone enjoys.

9. You successfully find your way around an unfamiliar city.

10. You buy someone a present which they really like.

Add up your total and you should have a percentage: 0–40 indicates pessimism, 60–100 suggests optimism. The middle range is too hard to call on a simple test such as this.

In fact, research suggests that optimists generally do better in life, live longer and fulfil more of their ambitions. A study by the Mayo Clinic in the US over a thirty year period has discovered that optimists live 19 per cent longer than pessimists! Interestingly it seems that optimists tend to get things wrong more often, but then making mistakes is an essential part of taking risks. And crucially, optimists are less likely to give up. Cultivating a positive mindset will help your mind work better and help you achieve more. Of course, there are some situations when being overly optimistic may not be smart. An over-optimistic interpretation can be inappropriate if you are dealing with someone who is seriously upset or ill. And being too optimistic when planning your finances may simply mean you run out of money.

When it comes down to it, how we see the world depends to a significant degree on how we account for things that happen to us, what Seligman calls our "explanatory style". He talks of the 3Ps, permanence, pervasiveness and personalisation, which determine the degree of our positive outlook.

1. *Permanence* – A pessimist might cry "Things will *never* get better" where an optimist might say "This is a temporary setback; tomorrow is a new day."

2. *Personalisation* – When something goes wrong, pessimists tend to blame themselves. They can easily sink into depression, feel victimised and see a pattern of failure and bad luck. An optimist takes control of events and says "How can I get around this?"

3. *Pervasiveness* – A pessimist can easily allow a setback to spread right through their lives, affecting everything. Optimists tend to look on it as an isolated situation.

The 3Ps help to explain why people who seem to be similarly gifted can have very different dispositions towards handling a challenging situation. The good news is that you can learn how to adopt a different mindset and see the world through a positive window. While we may be born more or less positive, and while the environment in which we operate undoubtedly influences us, we *can* influence our attitude to change. Any descriptive phrases that we may apply to ourselves, whether at the pioneer or at the stay-at-home end of the spectrum, are not fixed like our blood group is fixed at birth. We *can* learn new ways of talking and thinking about situations.

A growth mindset

While maintaining optimism is key to our ability to be open to change, even more important is the way we see our potential for achievement. Specifically, the degree to which we believe that we can grow and develop – that we can, in a sense, get smarter if we invest our effort – hugely determines any decision we might want to take about whether to invest our effort in something. It is easy to see the evolutionary reason for this; if we believe we are already about as intelligent as we are likely to get then there may seem little point in working hard to get smarter!

Two people have led thinking in this area. The first, David Perkins, has coined the phrase "learnable intelligence" to encapsulate his ideas. Perkins has demonstrated that it really is possible for students to learn how to become more intelligent. This concept is, at first, a counterintuitive one for anyone who has grown up assuming that, wherever they sit on the nature vs. nurture argument, intelligence is largely a fixed commodity. But stop and think how a different approach might change the way a student sees his or her time at school or college. The following table, based on an adaptation by Learning and Teaching Scotland of work by Harvard researcher David Perkins, is currently being promoted in schools.

Ability matters most	It's effort that makes the difference
Understanding is something that just happens	Understanding usually comes gradually, a bit at a time
If you are smart you get it, if you are not you don't	You can understand a little or a lot; you can never understand anything completely
If you don't catch on quickly, you might as well give up for the present at any rate	Some people take longer to learn than others – even fast learners don't always catch on right away
Effort won't get you far; ability is what really counts	To understand you often have to hang in there and persist
If you are not bright enough, there's not much anyone can do to help you	Success in learning depends as much on effort as on ability
If you can't do something, then it's because you're not up to it	If you can't do something it's likely to be because you're not trying hard enough or you're not getting the right kind of help

Source: www.ltscotland.org

The idea that intelligence is learnable has not yet gained wide acceptance. Indeed it is contested by some scientists. It is a cultural idea or meme that has not yet won out evolutionarily. Once upon a time we thought that in any one tribe some would be smart, strong hunters and would survive, while others would be less so and might not thrive. IQ conveniently reinforced this simplistic view of human ability and we have lived with the consequence for a century. But even a sceptic might concede that, just as our brains have evolved biologically, with a big spurt during the period when we learned how to use language and "become" Homo sapiens, so it is reasonable to imagine some kind of cultural evolution of the mind as we live on an increasingly crowded and complex planet.

A second major influence on this kind of thinking is Carol Dweck. She has gone beyond schools into homes and workplaces with her powerful and increasingly well-supported message about the importance of a growth mindset. In terms of dealing with change effectively, those with a growth mindset are much likely to accept and even relish new experiences. For these are bound to provide an opportunity for learning and development. Fixed mindset people are likely to be threatened by change, worrying that in new circumstances they may not be able to demonstrate their ability. Those with a growth outlook will be formulating questions: What can I learn? How can I do it better? What will I need to help me? How can I help other people? And so on. Most significantly, Dweck has shown how it is possible to change your mindset.

At its simplest level Dweck's approach changes conversations, both those we have with others and the ones we carry on in our own heads. We stop remarking on people's cleverness and start noticing the things that they do to improve. Our own inner talk shifts too. We focus more on the process of learning, on the things we can do that will help us to improve.

Interestingly, the man credited with the invention of the kind of tests that led to IQ, Alfred Binet, also believed that intelligence was learnable. He described the idea that intelligence is fixed as a "brutal pessimism" and pointed out that it is possible to improve attention, memory and judgement, all components of what it is to be smart.

To sum up, when it comes to dealing with change, while there are aspects of individual personality which tend to make us more or less disposed to it, mindset is a more powerful indicator. And whereas personality is relatively stable, mindset can be altered if we want to change it.

Habits of mind and patterns of action

In Rule 1 we saw how our minds have the capacity both to explore and make new connections, as well as the tendency to organise our insights and learning into patterns. Such pattern-making, while essential as a means of dealing with huge amounts of data and experience, becomes our way of seeing the world. It is all too easy to get stuck in a particular way of doing or being. Perhaps because we have expended effort in establishing it in the first place there is an evolutionary reluctance to squander our efforts. But in a rapidly changing world not to be ready, willing and able to change is clearly not a smart position to adopt.

Luckily we can all get better at being open to change, but only if we really want to and if we are prepared to cultivate certain habits of mind.

Reframing

In the examples from Seligman's work on explanatory style it was clear that the same event could be interpreted in different ways. Let's suppose that a photocopier breaks down as you rush to make copies of an important document for a meeting. In terms of personalisation you have a choice. Either you can account for this mechanical failure as part of a wider pattern of actions which disadvantage you. Taxis never stop. You often miss the last bus home. You never get served at a bar. Your children are always letting you down. And so forth. Or you can inject some critical detachment and conclude that, for good practical reasons – the paper jammed, there was not enough toner, you pressed the wrong buttons in your rush – your attempt to make copies was not successful.

Tool: The 3Ps in practice

Next time something adverse or surprising happens to you try these prompt questions:

- *Permanence* – Is this going to last forever or can I change it or the way I see it? Will it always happen like this or can I do something differently?

- *Personalisation* – What caused this? Look around and come up with at least three practical reasons why it has not just happened to you! Depersonalise!

- *Pervasiveness* – Will this affect every aspect of your life? Think about the other aspects of your life where it would have turned out differently. In other words, don't assume that just because it went wrong in this situation you will be similarly affected in other aspects of your life!

In other words how you frame any event really matters. Psychotherapists have long known this and this technique is widely taught to people who have become locked in limiting or negative views of themselves. In such circumstances it is helpful for someone to find another way of seeing their situation, one that will be more positive and esteem-boosting for him or her. Politicians also make regular use of this technique. Even when they have just lost an election they manage to put a positive spin on it, insisting, for example, that they won more votes than last time or that their opponents did worse than expected. Famously in the US presidential election campaign in 1984, when there was some concern about Ronald Reagan's age, Reagan quipped to his opponent Walter Mondale: "I will not make age an issue of this campaign. I am not going to exploit, for political purposes, my opponent's youth and inexperience." In one deft sentence Reagan reframed the issue so that voters could see his age as an asset (in terms of his experience) rather than as a liability.

Indeed getting into the habit of reframing situations can be seen most readily in the language we choose to describe what happens to us. When we face a difficult issue we can either describe it as a problem or a challenge. When things go wrong we can see something as a mistake or a genuine opportunity to learn. When someone criticises us we can either bridle with anger or develop a capacity to thank them for their feedback and then go on to reflect on the degree to which what we have been told is true or not.

And at the core of our world view, if we hold on to the idea that we are able to grow and develop, then, as Carol Dweck has shown, we are likely to see the expenditure of effort as part of our continuing evolution and be looking for new ways of approaching the issues we face rather than assuming that we have reached the limits of our potential.

Inquiring

If we are set on fulfilling our potential then we need constantly to be asking questions. This is the main way we have of establishing whether, when we face a new situation, a course of action is sensible or not. It's long been accepted that asking questions is an important aspect of what it is to be creative and intelligent. Yet we know that, as we grow older we gradually stop asking so many questions. Some argue that this is because we begin to know more and therefore need to ask less. But in reality questions breed questions. And as the speed of change continues to increase there are more and more things that we might like to find out.

Some organisations have begun to enshrine the habit of inquiring by establishing structures which empower all employees to learn how to undertake mini-enquiries of their own. This is becoming increasingly popular in both education and health care in the UK and the US (incidentally, I am deliberately using both the British English (enquiry) and the US English (inquiry) throughout this Rule!). Frequently organisations use a form of what is sometimes referred to as the PDSA cycle:

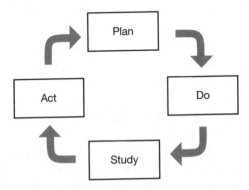

This cycle was widely popularised by W. Edwards Deming, the guru of the quality improvement movement,

and is used in a range of contexts from automobile manu-
facturing (where it began in Japan) and mobile phones, to
the public sector and third sector. The cycle invites us first
of all to notice something that is not currently working to
best effect. We then plan a small intervention that we believe
might improve the situation. (An example in a hospital
might focus on the way patients are contacted for routine
appointments which is often inefficient and leads to people
not attending.) At every stage we are invited to enquire.
(How many people currently do not turn up? Why don't we
remind them a day beforehand by text message?)

Based on the answers we get, a *plan* is made which will
try out a different way of approaching the issue. (We'll let
patients choose the time within options we give them. We'll
take their e-mail and mobile telephone numbers. We'll send
an automated reminder by e-mail and text.) At this stage
we may be wanting to ask questions such as: How will we
know if what we are proposing is working any better? (A
simple "percentage attending appointments" under the new
approach compared to the percentage in previous months
might suffice in this example.)

Then we will try out (*do*) the new system for a short
period, say a month and measure (*study*) the difference. (Not
all examples will be reducible to numbers as this is one is.)
Finally we will *act* differently in the light of what we find
out, putting into practice those elements which work and
refining those which need more thought.

A process like PDSA helps to make inquiry a way of life
in an organisation. (You can read more about how this can
be further embedded as a pattern of social interaction in
Rule 8.) This particular approach is a very explicit one. Some
may prefer just to have the idea of inquiry spinning away in
the back of their minds, rather like the way Isaac Newton
does when he says "I keep the subject of my enquiry constantly before me, and wait till the first dawning opens

gradually, by little and little, into a full and clear light." As we found earlier on in Rule 3, we do not need to strain at the leash all the time for our questions to be answered!

Tool – PDSA

Use the PDSA approach on a challenge you are currently facing. Take the chance to test out your thinking before having to commit to it!

In today's Internet-dominated world there is a particular aspect of our enquiry which each of us tends to rely on. It can be summed up by its eponym, Google. On the World Wide Web we can Google anything. And therein lies a problem. Attractive as the concept of searching – a kind of inquiry – seems to be, it is all too easy to suspend our questioning brain and graze on the smorgasbord of intellectual food that exists on the Internet. In many ways it is not so much searching as researching that we need to be good at. For it is all too easy to take at face value something that seems to match our initial search. What do we know about the site? How reliable is it or does it seem to be? How do we know?

This assumes that we find what we are looking for! More often than not it is the conceptualising of the search itself which makes it more or less likely that we will find what we want. These three searches about searching on the web make the point.

Search on Google about how to search the web and you get hugely different amounts of data as the following numbers of possible results shows:

Search words	Results
Search web	488,000,000
Search web effectively	2,370,000
"Search web effectively"	6

The first search is framed far too broadly and the third is far too restrictive. And as any skilled web searcher knows I have not used any of the other signals and words which would help me further refine and deepen my search. Apply some simple Boolean principles of symbolic logic (named after the nineteenth century mathematician George Boole) and use terms like AND, OR and AND NOT, and the likelihood of a search being relevant rises dramatically. Make sure that you identify six or so key words, normally nouns, and make judicious use of " " and web inquiry can become increasingly refined.

You will of course have to bring your enquiring mind to bear as to the reliability of anything that you find.

Living with uncertainty

In Rule 1 we looked at the way the mind loves the clarity of patterns. It constantly seeks to make order out of chaos. Indeed it craves that which it can predict and know. As I write we are in the middle of a major financial crisis, with banks being bailed out by national governments and all of the normal certainties about markets, currency values and interest rates being turned upside down. No one really knows what to do. Fixed interest financial products guaranteed or linked to the government are favoured by most people as they seem safest. In times of the greatest uncertainty we favour safety. But given that we really do not know what is going to happen, once we have made any prudent changes to the way we manage our money, it is really not worth expending energy worrying about it. We need, in short, to live sufficiently in the present and focus on what's going well and what we already have some degree of control over. (In the case of the financial crisis there might be a whole series of good things going on which have nothing to do with money, along with a small series of practical steps that can be taken to narrow the odds of you losing your money.)

Of course, this is easy to say and often difficult to do. The habits of mind that make us able to live with uncertainty also involve the ability to look not just to the present, but also backwards and forwards. We can look back systemically and see that there have always been cycles of change which have included financial bust and boom. Or, perhaps more pertinently, we can recall situations when we did not know what to do in the past and remind ourselves that we were in fact resourceful enough to come up with some ways of dealing with it. We can look forwards, consciously encouraging our minds to explore different potential scenarios.

But at the core of it all we need to cultivate an openness to change born of confidence that, as an evolved being, we have various strategies to deploy whenever we meet a new situation. (We will explore the idea of adaptive intelligence more in Rule 5.) Once we realise that we can, to a large extent, choose the way we look at the world, we have essentially adopted a helpful philosophical position. Bertrand Russell summed it up as follows: "To teach how to live with uncertainty, yet without being paralysed by hesitation, is perhaps the chief thing that philosophy can do."

Self-discipline

We have already seen how self-discipline in terms of delayed gratification is an indicator of success (the "marshmallow test" described in Rule 3). But to create enough order and control in turbulent times also involves some broader areas of self-regulation. Albert Bandura has contributed some important thinking here. In *Self-Efficacy in Changing Societies* and many other books he has helpfully defined self-regulation as having three components:

1. Self-observation – the capacity to look at ourselves and keep track of what we do.

2. Judgement – comparing ourselves with an external standard, either set by us or by others.

3. Self-response – according to how well we do in (2) we feel good or bad and reward or punish ourselves.

Of course, these three components are interrelated and virtually no one regulates his or her life according to such explicit categories anyway! But underlying Bandura's thinking is the assumption that, however we calculate it, self-regulated people are capable of setting and holding to goals that matter to them. Providing the goal still remains achievable, then when we stray from it the dissatisfaction this causes can act as a spur to us re-engaging with a task. If the goal slips too far out of our grasp, then the discrepancy may seem too great and lead to us giving up.

As a result of this kind of thinking it is important during a period of rapid change to be able both to hold on to our overarching objective and modify our more short-term goals in the light of this, which requires both fixity of purpose and flexibility. In truth, while there is some evidence that you can practise some aspects of this, not enough is known about how we can get better at being self-regulated. There is a wealth of evidence that setting achievable short-term, specific goals is beneficial. But as to how we develop the habits of mind which are likely to allow us both to be robust enough not to be blown off course but also responsive enough to change our methods, more work needs to be done.

Appreciative Inquiry

In terms of the kinds of patterns of social interaction which work best when dealing with change, one approach is increasingly demonstrating its value. Appreciative Inquiry (AI) is a relatively new way of managing change in organisations. Created by David Cooperrider and colleagues at Case Western Reserve University, AI is revolutionising the way change is being organised. Traditionally groups of people respond to an external challenge by looking at the gap between what they need to do to meet a new challenge in the external environment and the organisational capability they see themselves as having. This is a kind of deficit model which tends to lead to the identification of a number of things which the organisation does not currently have. As a result when individuals in the organisation are told this they are likely to be both defensive and fearful. Change is immediately framed as "a problem to be fixed" and the organisation tends to label itself as "not being up to a challenge".

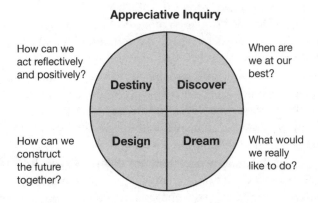

Appreciative Inquiry

How can we act reflectively and positively? — Destiny

When are we at our best? — Discover

How can we construct the future together? — Design

What would we really like to do? — Dream

By contrast the AI model is quite different. It assumes that organisations have many strengths which they can harness to meet any number of challenges. The trick, therefore, is to catch the organisation when it is working at its best.

Rather than problematising issues, the first of a four part process is to discover what happens when the organisation and individuals within it are working really well. This process normally involves a series of interviews, the products of which are stories and lists of contextualised strengths. Employees might be asked:

> What are you most proud of?
> What do we do best?
> Which are our best services?
> Which are our best products?
> Which are our strongest relationships?

The rule for any interview is that is has to be wholly positive. For some people this is surprisingly difficult. You are not saying that people cannot talk about what is not going well. Rather you are just framing the discussion so that when they do move into this mode they approach it having confirmed all the many good things they are doing. Each of these questions then prompts a story.

From Discover you then move on to Dream. This invites individuals to create a wish-list of what they would like to do if time, money and people were infinitely available and whichever unwelcome circumstances are currently dominating their thinking are magically removed. This part of the process frees people's minds from "I can't do x because …" by creating a framework within which they can simply dream on, sharing their most fervent hopes.

Once the first two stages are complete you have an agenda for action and for change. You have reminded yourself and your colleagues what you are already good at and laid out your real agenda. It is real because none of the normal organisational excuses for inaction – resources of all kinds – can be cited as a reason for *not* undertaking a particular course of action!

Tool – Three wishes

Apply the Dream element of AI to something you are grappling with.

Imagine you are constrained by neither time nor money. Imagine you had three wishes. Now dream on. What would you like to do?

What would you really like to do?

What would you really, really like to do?

The three wishes tool forces us to stop hiding behind the practical limitations of life and enables us to be supremely positive and aspirational.

The remaining two parts of the process are relatively traditional. But they will be done positively and framed by the Discover and Design elements. Some people find the fourth element Destiny too folksy, in which case you can always just substitute the much simpler Deliver. In terms of social interaction, AI promotes questioning, dialogue, creativity and, most importantly in terms of all of the issues we have been exploring in this Rule, a collective mentality of growth. It is an ideal social process to ensure that members of an organisation really see that they cannot only change the way they see the world – they can also substantially influence any course of action by the way in which such change is determined and agreed.

Rule 4 – The argument so far

While we are all different and some of us may exhibit a higher appetite for risk and a more instinctive tolerance for uncertainty, we can all change the way we see the world. For too long we have seen personality and events as being, respectively, fixed and inevitable. The ability to rethink our view of and response to any situation is something that human beings have learned but do not always practise. In all aspects of our lives, not just when it comes to dealing with change, there is considerable benefit to be derived from being able to see our surroundings through a positive lens. And this does not mean that we need to suspend our critical faculties. Far from it. In a data-rich world when we may often feel that we are swimming in too much information, we need to refine and sharpen our ability to sift the wheat from the chaff and also to be clear about the status of any data we may have found.

Habits of mind connected with this which may be of particular interest to us include reframing, inquiring, self-discipline and being able to live with uncertainty. And we may wish to learn how to be more appreciative.

Last words:

> What we call the beginning is often the end
> And to make an end is to make a beginning.
> The end is where we start from.

> T. S. Eliot, "Little Gidding", *The Four Quartets*

Rule 5 – We can all learn how to change more effectively

Adapt or perish, now as ever, is nature's inexorable imperative.

H. G. Wells

Adaptive intelligence

Every time I learn something it pushes some old stuff out of my brain.

Homer Simpson

One hundred and fifty years ago, as the quotation from Charles Darwin which begins *rEvolution* makes clear, a compelling case was made for responsiveness to change (rather than, say, cleverness or strength) being the critical success factor in natural selection. Of course, as Darwin was not looking at the evolution of human beings he does not explore what people who thrive in today's changing ecosystem actually *do* that is different.

What habits of mind and patterns of social interaction characterise what I am calling adaptive intelligence? This question will be at the heart of this Rule just as Rule 5 – that we can all learn how to change more effectively – is at the core of the argument of this book. Of course, while we can all learn how to adapt more effectively, some will learn this more effectively than others. That's natural selection. But my supposition is that, if we really want to adapt, then there are some practical things that we can all do which will help most of us.

In this Rule we will explore some of the elements of responsiveness – what happens when action and reflection combine so that you act differently as a consequence. Many people are either strong on action or on reflection but not on both. But to be responsive we need both these capabilities along with a determination to learn from experience and do things differently.

It was psychologist Jean Piaget who first suggested that learning is really a process of adaptation. He talked of two processes at work, "accommodation" and "assimilation". We notice something, adjust our thinking and, as a consequence, adapt the way we act. In practice, we either fit our theory to our experience, accommodation, or fit our experience to any theory we have already formed in our head, assimilation.

So, if your theory of children is that they are always naughty and you meet a child who is well behaved, you would accommodate your views by adjusting your theory. From then on children would become capable of good or bad behaviour. If you chose to assimilate this data, then your view of children would remain the same and your mind would explain away your experience by thinking of the nice child as an odd exception to the rule.

Of the two kinds of adaptation described by Piaget, accommodation is the more challenging for it requires us to rethink the way we view the world. Assimilation occurs when we are able to fit our experience to a theory we have developed. So, for example, as we grow up we discover the force of gravity. As a baby we push our milk bottle off the high chair and it falls to the floor. The same happens for bits of fruit. Then we play with a hose and see the water arching downwards. Footballs, glass, even human beings all gradually get assimilated into our initially sketchy sense of the force of gravity.

Intelligent learners, according to Piaget, know when to accommodate and when to assimilate. They know "what to do when they don't know what to do"!

Of course, to begin the process of adaptation at all you have to notice what is going on in the first place. And it turns out that the brain has evolved to be surprisingly lazy at noticing. Here's a simplified version of an entertaining card trick by Andy Bauch which makes the point. Try it out for yourself.

Look at these cards and choose one card. Concentrate on it very hard so you will be sure to remember it. Amazingly I know just which card you have chosen and I am going to remove it. Turn to the end of this Rule to see just how I will do this.

Just for a fleeting second most people are fooled; I certainly was the first time I tried it!

The brain is surprisingly selective in what it thinks it has seen. Even a simple instruction – "Concentrate on it very hard" – can be "misheard" to mean "Don't bother about the other cards". Our minds tend to overestimate what they can take in with a single look.

There are many other experiments that make this point. Daniel Simons and Christopher Chabris at Harvard created a classic experiment involving a film of a handful of people playing basketball. Subjects are asked to count the passes made by one of the teams as they watch. But unbeknown to them a woman dressed in a gorilla suit walks across the screen, at one stage even turning to the camera and thumping her chest. About half of the watchers failed to spot a woman dressed in a gorilla suit even though she has walked slowly across the scene for nine seconds. The gorilla experiment is a classic example of another kind of inattentional blindness.

Neuroscientists also have another useful concept, plasticity. This describes the way that the brain reorganises itself and changes as the result of experience. Scientists have known for some while about the amazing capacity of the brain, when damaged, to enrol parts which are not normally involved in specific brain functions. This phenomenon is particularly evident in some stroke victims who are initially paralysed but are able to recover some movement as another part of their brain takes over. But plasticity is also increasingly being used to discuss the more fundamental ways in which our brains continue to develop and evolve. The old maxim "use it or lose it" is not helpful because even older people have the capacity to make new synaptic connections. As Marvin Minsky, author of *The Society of Mind*, says: "The principal activities of brains are making changes in themselves."

A useful strand of thinking about effective adaption has been developed by Giyoo Hatano and Kayoko Inagaki. They have coined the term "adaptive expertise" to describe capability that is beyond routine expertise. To illustrate this simply someone may be routinely able to cook bacon and eggs for breakfast and make baked beans on toast for supper with great confidence, but given a set of novel ingredients may find it more difficult to adapt what they know to help them create a delicious meal. Adaptive experts are adept at creating new procedures and methods in novel situations, drawing on what they have learned in other domains.

It seems likely that acquiring adaptive expertise requires significant time and a degree of confidence in a significant number of core concepts on which the learner can build to create new ways of dealing with an issue or situation. Certainly it will help if there are regular opportunities to experience new situations and exposure, in a safe environment, to ideas which are challenging and different.

One of the key determinants of successful adaptation is the ability to transfer learning from one aspect of your life to another. Indeed the ability of human beings to transfer their learning from one domain to another is the Holy Grail of successful adaptation. So, in our tribal days we might have learned something about cooperation while hunting a woolly mammoth which we could then apply back in the cave to help us make a meal together with the rest of the tribe. Or, in today's world, we might learn something about anger management on a course at work and then effortlessly incorporate it in our relationship with our partner. If only it were so easy!

American psychologists Mary Gick and Keith Holyoak use this example to help students understand more about the transfer of knowledge. Consider the following problem:

> Imagine you were a doctor faced with a patient who has an inoperable stomach tumour. You have at your disposal rays that can destroy human tissue when directed with sufficient intensity. At lower intensity the rays are harmless to healthy tissue, but they do not affect the tumour either. How can you use these rays to destroy the tumour without destroying the surrounding healthy tissue?

Few students find it easy to solve this problem. But the majority (90 per cent) are able to do so when they are also given this passage and told to use the information in it to help them:

> A general wishes to capture a fortress located in the centre of a country. There are many roads radiating outwards from the fortress. All have been mined so that while groups of men can pass over the roads safely, a large force will detonate the mines. A

full-scale direct attack is therefore impossible. The general's solution is to divide his army into small groups, send each group to the head of a different road and have the groups converge simultaneously on the fortress.

The students are able to see the analogy between dividing up the troops into small groups and using a number of small doses of radiation which converge on the same area of the tumour. But they do much better when the explicit connection between the two bits of information has been pointed out.

Researcher David Perkins is particularly insightful here, too. With his colleague Gavriel Salomon he distinguishes between two kinds transfer, "low road" and "high road". Low road transfer occurs when a new context spontaneously reminds you of an earlier experience. A good example would be the first use of a new mobile phone. Although not identical to your last one, you easily transfer your knowledge of previous phones and rapidly adjust to using your new one. A similar example would be driving a new car or even driving a small van when you are normally a car driver. The situation has enough clues and correspondences in it to prompt you to act in the right way. Your "reading" of the new context is essentially a reflex reaction and largely non-conscious (although you may need to briefly stop to check your intuitive reactions).

High road transfer is different. It takes place when you more consciously seek to dredge up and apply things you have learned in contexts which may be quite different from the one you now find yourself in. Maybe you were taught to count to ten when you hurt yourself as a child (as a means of making it less likely that you would scream out in agony). Years later you find yourself sitting in a meeting and, infuriated by the wilful disagreeableness of a colleague, you are about to shout something rude at them when you feel prompted to try something you have not used for many a long year. After a moment's thought you quietly start counting to ten and, after doing so, you find that your anger has subsided sufficiently for you to concentrate on the issue at hand and ignore your irritating colleague. Somehow you have found the wherewithal to avoid an embarrassing situation! High road transfer requires us to use our adaptive intelligence and apply what we have learned from an earlier situation.

Transferring knowledge is a complex matter. Context and environment matter to the extent that every situation is different. Successful learning transfer seems to depend on a number of factors, including:

- Having enough knowledge before trying to use it elsewhere – for example, by making sure you are really confident about your presentation skills in front of your family before you try it at a conference.

- Significant time spent practising in different situations before trying it elsewhere – for example, deliberately practising sight-reading music over a period of time before volunteering to play the piano for your local choir.

- When the tasks share some common elements – for example, learning Spanish after learning Latin, when you have already grasped some key principles of the way languages work.

- Organising information into some kind of pattern or conceptual framework – for example, having a clear idea of how you remember things so that you can apply key techniques to help you memorise a complex argument for use in an important meeting.

• Learning similar content in different situations – for example, learning how to introduce yourself effectively at home with your family, with friends and at school.

Learning about learning

In the US, John Bransford and his colleagues on the Committee on Developments in the Science of Learning have made a powerful case for one of the key elements of successful knowledge transfer (and therefore, by implication, adaptation) being the degree to which learners are more aware of themselves as learners and thinkers. Clearly we all bring some element of prior learning to most situations which we encounter. But the more we are able to bring it to the surface of our understanding of what may be going on, the better we are likely to be able to do it. In fact, the more we can consciously talk about what and how we are learning the better. If I do this, I wonder if that would happen? What was it about the way I dealt with her that seemed to work? What did I do the last time I encountered a situation like this? What else could I try?

The idea that to ensure the successful continuing adaptation of the species we might want to teach children how to learn is something that I have personally, with Guy Claxton, all those associated with the UK's Campaign for Learning, with the Royal Society of Arts' Opening Minds and with a growing number of UK educators, been very much associated. In a sense there is (sadly) nothing new in this. Fifty years ago John Holt, for example, was arguing that: "Since we cannot know what knowledge they will need, it is senseless to try to teach it in advance. Instead our job must be to turn out people who love learning so much, and who learn so well, that they will be able to learn whatever needs to be learned."

Notions like these are at the heart of adaptive intelligence. Where once we thought that intelligence was largely fixed at birth and mainly concerned with the ability to use a relatively limited range of general cognitive skills of the kind traditionally measured by IQ, we now know that this is not the case.

So far in *rEvolution* we have touched on various approaches to intelligence which contain useful learning for us as we seek to thrive in times of change. Indeed in the last twenty years there has been a huge amount of activity in this field, ushered in by Howard Gardner's notion of multiple intelligences. The idea that intelligence is multidimensional, although difficult to prove and harder still to measure in any reliable way (as IQ can be, for example), is intuitively true for most people. It just seems common sense that you can be talented in different domains. Gardner's thinking is not unlike the kinds of approach adopted by William James in *The Principles of Psychology* when he wrote: "Most people live, whether physically, intellectually or morally, in a very restricted circle of their potential being. They make very small use of their possible consciousness and of their soul's resource in general." Gardner and James give us an agenda for our own self-actualisation and a framework for talking about the different ways in which we might develop.

Robert Sternberg has gone further to develop the concept of successful intelligence. (It's worth noting at this point that there's a bit of an industry in coining new kinds of intelligence and you may think that "successful" is a step too far!) Sternberg usefully hones in on what he calls practical and creative intelligence. It is this, he argues, which predicts our ability to adapt and thrive in the real world. People who are successful "know their strengths; they know their weaknesses. They capitalise on their strengths; they compensate for or correct their weaknesses."

The Darwinian echoes are easy to hear. Sternberg tells an amusing evolutionary story to make his point which I paraphrase here.

> Two teenagers are walking through a forest. (For reasons of political correctness you can decide whether they are two boys or two girls, but they need to be the same gender!) One is a conventionally able student who gets good grades in tests at school. The second is different. He regularly fails at school and is at best thought to be savvy or street smart. Suddenly a huge, hungry grizzly bear appears out of nowhere. The first student, calculating that the bear will overtake him in sixteen seconds, begins to panic. The second actor in our drama is, meanwhile, coolly taking off his walking boots and replacing them with trainers from his backpack. "You must be mad", says the first child, "we'll never run fast enough to escape the bear." "No," replies the second, "good point. But all I have to do is to outrun you!" And with that he races off leaving the first student as a potential snack for the bear.

Stories like this remind us that in fiction, as in life, it is often the more practically minded and creative individuals who survive and thrive!

Another interesting notion is that the technology we are creating is making us more intelligent. Think of your own life for a moment. If you have a laptop and have ever lost it or had its hard disk crash, how did that affect you? Or if you own a mobile phone or some kind of hand-held device like a Blackberry and you lost it, how did that impact on your ability to function?

For most of us such events can be not unlike suffering a mild stroke. We suddenly find ourselves deprived of a crucial part of our "brain". So, what role do electronic computing "brains" play in our lives? Can they be said to be an aspect of our intelligence and part of our ability to adapt?

Many people think that they can. What, they might argue, is the difference between humankind's early forays into flint and then metal toolmaking, or his invention of the wheel and his more recent use of silicon chips in small computers? We are, as Andy Clark has argued, cyborgs, hybrids, part-man, part-machine: "For what is special about human brains, and what best explains the distinctive features of human intelligence, is precisely their ability to enter into deeper and complex relationships with nonbiological constructs, props and aids."

We are simply doing what our forebears did but in an age of intelligent computers. Indeed those who use Blackberries and other hand-held tools best maintain that they give them a wonderful evolutionary advantage over we mere mortals dependent on being attached to Google via an old-fashioned computer. For they can rove the world answering questions from their work colleagues or family while, in theory at least, climbing Everest or sailing around the globe. If they are lost, they can simply summon up Google Earth or any of the many other mapping applications, relying on an in-built GPS feature to help them know where they are at any given moment. We have become so smart that, while we are in cyborg mode, we can no longer get lost wherever we are on the planet. (Other unintended consequences can also be a total inability to slow down and switch off and an irritating ability never to concentrate on one task or human conversation for more than a second.)

As well as technology, there is a new generation of mind-expanding drugs which can also boost our intelligence and capacity to adapt. Neuroscientists believe that we are about to enter an era when a new generation of smart drugs will be able to "cure" such terrible diseases as Alzheimer's. Ritalin, for example, is already widely prescribed to deal with attention deficit disorder and Prozac to combat the effects of depression. Other drugs are now available or being developed which will allow us to improve our memory and attentiveness. Are these legitimate mind tools? Have you ever kept yourself awake when driving or completing an important assignment late at night by drinking coffee? If so, what's the difference between caffeine and Ritalin and co.? Notwithstanding the huge ethical issues this raises (Is it cheating to take smart drugs during examinations? Does an aspirin taken to reduce a headache count in this category? Is there any difference between a smart drug and a smart tool for remembering, such as mnemonic?) clearly we can ingest man-made substances just as we can use man-made devices which make us better at adapting.

And then, of course, there is the issue of language. Arguably our greatest discovery, our ability to communicate with words, has transformed Homo sapiens. Psychologist Steven Pinker has coined an interesting word to describe us. Not herbivores or even omnivores, he sees Homo sapiens as "verbivores". Not only do words give us the ability to communicate, but also, crucially, the ability to think and record both the process and outcomes of our thoughts in speech and writing.

Indeed a group of which I am part in the UK, The English Project, has hypothesised that most words are coined in the home to meet a new need. In *Kitchen Table Lingo*, they share some of the hundreds of words generated by people from all over the world. The words are a living testimony to the creativity of people.

Humans are the only species with language. Indeed Daniel Dennett has suggested that our ability to use language is in both a philosophical and a very real sense our most powerful mind tool. There is no limit to what we can imagine in our mind's eye with a combination of words and images. Words to us are like the termite's complex constructions built out of mud or the beaver's carefully gnawed wooden houses.

Our ability to use language creates enormous pleasure and provides us with an enduringly important ability, the telling of stories and the recording of our collective memory as history. But it has, according to Pinker, given us an even greater evolutionary advantage. It has given us what he called "generate-and-test". You can call this science if you like, or you can see it as the science of making mistakes and learning from them. For, as life zooms on, with words we can contemplate stuff that happens, extracting the meaning from it so that we can adapt and do it differently next time. This "puts our minds on a different plane from the minds of our nearest relatives among the animals. This species-specific process of enhancement has become so swift and powerful that a generation of its design improvements can now dwarf the R-and-D efforts of millions of years of evolution by natural selection."

And just as we see technologies evolving rapidly at the moment we should not underestimate our capacity to develop and express our ideas and our comprehension of life on earth in ever more sophisticated language.

Houston, we have a problem

Astronaut Jim Lovell's infamous description of a potentially life-threatening disaster on board Apollo 13 has entered the popular lexicon. Indeed the actions of the Apollo 13 crew have come to be synonymous with creative problem-solving. Fifty-five hours into the flight a cryogenic tank in the service module, one of three modules making up the spacecraft, exploded. What followed showed three men demonstrating high levels of adaptive intelligence under enormous pressure. Their challenge became a simple one: how to get back to earth safely. From being a mission to the moon, the first stage was to create a new and compelling goal – splashdown in the Pacific Ocean. Everything on board had to be reconsidered in this light; whether it could be adapted to serve a useful function in getting back to earth (where originally it had been designed for lunar landing).

So, the lunar landing module became the main cabin. An early task was to calculate the amount of energy they would need to achieve re-entry into the earth's atmosphere. Without a working on-board computer everything had to be relayed to those at Mission Control who then did the calculations for the astronauts. Indeed a parallel version of the spacecraft was set up so that scientists back on earth could use their creativity to come up with solutions using the same equipment as that available to the crew. Every item on board became potential problem-solving material. And the main challenge, conserving fuel, meant the crew choosing to endure freezing temperatures, sickness, thirst, a lack of sleep and radio silence to conserve energy.

In the constrained world of the spacecraft the crew began to explore the potential for adaptation of every piece of equipment and every system. After much ingenuity, suffice to say, the spacecraft splashed down safely using an incredible number of clever workarounds. In a sense this situation closely mimics some that our forebears must have had to face evolutionarily. Suddenly resources which had been plentiful became scarce. Those who survived were the most creative problem-solvers who were able to adapt quickly.

A crew with their spaceship is a very specific environment and the men on Apollo 13 had to deal with a set of very specific problems, hopefully ones that will never occur again. But if we think not of astronauts' working conditions but of the conditions that most of us find ourselves in during our daily working lives then we cannot simply rely on having three creative individuals, alongside the considerable resources of NASA, devoted to solving one specific problem!

Chris Argyris has distinguished between two ways of dealing with problems which he calls single- and double-loop learning.

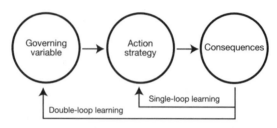

Single-loop learning is when a problem occurs that is fixed and no significant action is taken to ensure that the problem does not occur again. Double-loop learning, on the other hand, involves understanding the underlying system. Once an error is detected and corrected the organisation then modifies its systems so that it does not happen again.

Arygris's idea of double-loop learning was an important step along the way towards the idea of the learning organisation as suggested by Bob Garratt, Peter Senge and others. Senge, in particular, introduced the important idea of systems thinking, what he calls the "fifth discipline". Systems thinking is a way of seeing the whole picture – seeing interrelationships and patterns of change rather than isolated moments.

In a number of industries and, in particular, in health care, systems thinking is increasingly referred to as quality improvement. And at the heart of this set of disciplines is a sense that, in order to be able to embed improvement in any kind of systematic way, everyone involved needs to be clearer about what it is they are doing as part of the process. As W. Edwards Deming put it: "If you can't describe what you are doing as a process, you don't know what you're doing." (Actually I don't think Deming is always right. Sometimes, when we are in the flow, for example, we are not capable of standing outside ourselves so that we can describe what we are doing. By the same token an expert carver or dancer, for example, is not necessarily able to put their complex art into words. But somebody skilled watching them might at least be able to have a go.)

A core element of any improvement activity is questioning and enquiry, as we saw in Rule 4. This is especially the case when we are interested in improving any system. American educator John Dewey expounded his belief that the way human beings exemplify Darwin's evolutionary thinking is through a continuous process of trial and error. Over a long lifetime he developed his thinking, expressed perhaps most clearly in *Logic: Theory of Inquiry* towards the end of his life. Dewey brought two core human activities together, the ability to generate theories and the capacity to undertake practical action. He argued that, for too long, these had been separated. He encouraged the generation of propositions and their testing out in the real world as a necessary and holistic approach to enquiry and the only effective way of understanding the way in which we acquire knowledge.

In many ways Donald Schön took over from where Dewey left off. Schön called his development of Dewey's thinking "reflection in action". By this he meant the ability of professional people to combine action and reflection in their working lives, Schön shows the different ways in which it is possible to develop reflective techniques which can be used by practitioners while they are actually undertaking their work tasks. Reflection might be provided formally through the use of coaching or 360° feedback sessions or less formally by a range of methods such as learning logs or reflective reports of specific incidents. Dewey specifically contextualised his approaches by reference to his belief that the world was no longer in a stable state but was evolving fast: "The loss of the stable state means that our society and all of its institutions are in *continuous* processes of transformation. We cannot expect new stable states that will endure for our own lifetimes. We must learn to understand, guide, influence and manage these transformations … We must, in other words, become adept at learning."

A key means of becoming adept at learning, or developing adaptive intelligence, is the development of resourcefulness and a repertoire of examples and techniques to aid reflection in action. The notion of repertoire is a key aspect of this approach. Practitioners build up a collection of images, ideas, examples and actions that they can draw upon.

Groups of people using these techniques, and those described over the next few pages, start to create not just a learning organisation but an adaptive organisation, one that has the systems and processes in place to evolve and become more intelligent as it anticipates and responds to the external environment.

Habits of mind and patterns of action

If we want to adapt and thrive then certain habits of mind will particularly help us to develop adaptive expertise.

Imitating

Imitation, as Oscar Wilde famously said, is the highest form of flattery. It is also one of the most powerful habits that we can adopt to ensure that we pick up the best of what we see others around us doing. Imitation is also one of the oldest forms of learning we know, both in its formal incarnation, as apprenticeship, or less formally as "learning with Nellie". From the earliest years learning by watching others is the main way in which we learn to walk and talk, for example.

Interestingly, the field of neuroscience has begun to give tantalising glimpses of what may be going on in the brain while we are observing others. Special kinds of brain cells called "mirror neurons" exist which are not only activated when we are performing an action but also fire up when we watch others doing something similar. Our brains, it would seem, are wired to notice and imitate others. More than this, recent research suggests that not only do our brains notice what others are doing, and activate the neural circuits we might use if we were performing the same action, they are also able to work out the intentions of those enacting what they see. We do not just imitate what they see; we also discern the purpose behind what we observe and take that into account in determining when, if and how to copy it.

In psychology there is also a field of research known as "social contagion" which seeks to explain the way in which behaviour can be "caught" (like a contagious disease) merely by being exposed to other people. Two kinds of behaviour can be caught in this way: the first can be summed up by the word "mood" and the second by "behaviour". We sense the mood of a group and find ourselves caught up in it. Or we experience certain behaviours – an excess of friendliness or hostility, for example – and act accordingly.

Of course, to imitate we have to notice in the first place and not get distracted or thrown off the scent as we saw on page 117 of this Rule! And there's noticing and noticing. We can look at someone demonstrating enormous skill managing a team of people through a mixture of judicious goal-setting and the giving of timely and actionable feedback, but if all we have seen is a group of people performing well then we have not really been noticing. Real noticing is seeing patterns and trends and exercising our judgement as we do so. In this example, having noticed specific patterns of behaviour, we will then want to try them out for ourselves and reflect on their effectiveness. By contrast, if what we have been watching seems to be an example of poor performance, then intelligent imitators will consciously want to try something different!

A simple if obvious way of maximising the likelihood of us learning by imitation is actively to seek and hang out with talented people. In terms of a lifetime of successful adaptation, there are certain periods when this matters more than others. In chronological order these include:

- early childhood friends our parents "choose"

- school and preschool friends we choose

- the college or university crowd we spend most time with

- the people we model ourselves on in our first (and subsequent) jobs

- the particular friends we go through life valuing most

- and so on.

Experimenting

Very few great ideas arrive fully formed into someone's mind. Rarely do we want to do something and get it right first time. In the vast majority of cases it requires a considerable period of experimentation.

As a child we do this all the time. We drop things from our high chair, push towers of Lego bricks until they fall over and see how hard we can hit someone before they cry out. It's one of the main ways in which we make sense of the world.

As we get older we tend to experiment less. Partly we know more and so, perhaps, feel less need to experiment. Maybe there is also the fear of making mistakes and looking foolish to contend with. Yet if we are to grow and evolve we need to be constantly experimenting and pushing ourselves to the boundaries of what we know – for this is where the real learning takes place.

Psychologist Lev Vygotsky first gave this idea a curious if logical name, the "zone of proximal development". This is the gap between what we can do without help and what we can achieve with help. It is the "grow zone" at the edge of our competence and confidence where we need to experiment and try things out in order to find out more about what we are capable of. If you are an athlete this might involve a stretching goal to run the distance half a second faster. If a young child it might mean trying to ride your bike without stabilisers for a few metres from the safety of your father's arms to your mother's.

Tool – What if?

At the heart of experimenting is curiosity, a commodity which we know leaks out of us as we grow older if we are not careful.

What if, by practising open-ended questioning (and statements of wondering) we actually got into the habit of doing this and were, as a consequence, more likely to wonder about things and experiment as to how we might develop our ideas further?

What happens if ...?
I wonder whether ...?
If I do this will that happen?
Is there anything to stop us ...?
I'd really like to try ...
This feels a bit precarious but ...
How will I feel if ...?
Who else do I know who knows about this?
Is there a better way of doing it?

And so on.

They are also very much the kind of questions which will help if we are to develop the habit of experimenting.

On many occasions experimenting may seem relatively safe and enjoyable. But if we feel particularly challenged then our response may be close to the diagram on page 130. In this case, just as we might do if in a period of enforced change, the critical moment we will need to reach is when willingly trialling a new approach or method even if we find it beyond us to start with.

Creative problem-solving

Experimentation is often the first stage of problem-solving and, as the Apollo 13 example made clear, creative problem-solving is an essential attribute to possess in any life-threatening situation. It is also an important life skill with a capital S.

What it takes to be really innovative in dealing with problems has been the subject of much speculation over the past few decades and a key thinker in this period has been Edward de Bono. Particularly associated with de Bono is the idea of "lateral thinking". Coined in the 1960s, lateral or sideways thinking looks at problems with fresh eyes. It stresses the importance of perception and creativity in breaking up a problem into component parts in such a way that takes us away from logical step-by-step thinking so that its solution becomes apparent to us. De Bono is clear about the importance of this temperamental approach to life: "There is no doubt that creativity is the most important human resource of all. Without creativity, there would be no progress, and we would be forever repeating the same patterns."

Two classic de Bono mind tools are Plus, Minus, Interesting and Six Thinking Hats. Plus, Minus, Interesting involves "thinking in threes". When confronting an issue it enables us to see, from a standpoint other than our normal binary one, if it is a good or bad idea by considering a third category, "interesting".

Plus +	Minus -	Interesting ?

Think of any proposition or issue you are grappling with at the moment. In the first two columns list all of the positive or negative consequences. But in the third put those which are neither good or bad but merely interesting or intriguing. Many people find that simply by introducing a third category their mind is opened up to seeing possibilities rather than confirming their initial prejudice about something.

Six Thinking Hats invites us to consider even more perspectives. The approach is an excellent way of getting the most out of creative teams and is a gentle allusion to the saying "putting on your thinking cap". Widely used in organisations, it works like this: de Bono assumes that when a team is grappling with a problem, it may be helpful to be really clear about the different roles you can play. So he suggests that you wear six differently coloured hats and act according to the role that each one suggests.

- White = You introduce neutral facts, figures and information.

- Red = You put forward hunches, feeling and intuitions.

- Black = You are logical and negative.

- Yellow = You are logical and positive.

- Green = You constantly come up with creative ideas for taking things forward.

- Blue = You act as the conductor of the orchestra, concentrating on managing the process of coming up with ideas successfully.

There are all sorts of ways in which this can be used, but the simplest is just to play the roles that each hat suggests.

In a group situation there are other unintended benefits. Simply wearing coloured hats induces a light-hearted and playful approach, exactly the kind of mind state when good creative thinking can thrive. But the essential idea – that you can consciously "walk around a problem" adopting a different role – can be used even when we are on our own when we can deliberately adopt within our own head either a logical approach or a more intuitive one.

Taken in isolation both these techniques are simply interesting mind tools. But used regularly, and once part of a large repertoire of regularly used approaches, we are likely to find that our habit of mind when confronted with difficult issues is to approach them as if they can be solved – if only we are able to see beyond the established patterns of our thought.

Sometimes it pays to remember Albert Einstein's definition of insanity as "doing the same thing over and over again and expecting different results"!

Reflection in action

Learning and adapting is a process involving the processing of experience. Half a century ago David Kolb helpfully depicted it thus:

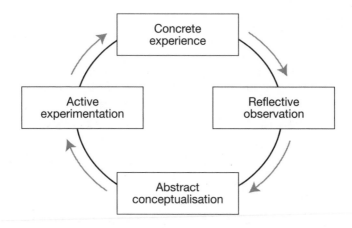

Successful adapters are constantly toggling between reflection and action. They experience something and bring their experimenting mind to bear on it both practically and more abstractly.

Peter Honey and Alan Mumford have developed well-established and much-used learning styles based on this powerful depiction of the learning process. Honey and Mumford turn the four moments of the learning process into the four habits of mind which might most often be associated with each aspect of the process – action, pragmatic activity, reflection and theorising, and personalise these as descriptors for different kinds of learning styles:

- *Activist.* Activists tend to immerse themselves in experiences. They will try anything once and are happy to give most things a go. They seem to thrive on the excitement of the here and now and are easily bored. They set great store by getting the job done.

- *Pragmatist.* Pragmatists like learning methods which encourage them to work on real issues and where they are shown techniques with an obvious practical benefit.

- *Reflector.* Reflectors normally enjoy learning methods which give them time to think and ponder, like keeping a journal. They like to be able to stand back from events and appreciate being given time to think before being plunged straight into a task. They enjoy writing reports. They tend not to like situations where they are forced to give instant responses or asked to act without enough data.

- *Theorist.* Theorists tend to enjoy learning which has a clear underlying concept or model. They like to be able to explore things methodically and enjoy structure. Although the learning may not be immediately relevant, theorists enjoy ideas and concepts. Theorists tend to be less comfortable when they are asked to express emotions or take part in activities which are open ended or deal with ambiguity.

Some people find that they have strong preferences when faced with certain tasks. So, given a new set of shelves to assemble from a box of parts we can imagine ourselves rushing to put them up by trial and error (activists) or spending a long time studying the instructions, checking that all the parts are there and then carefully putting them together step-by-step (theorists).

But our preference is only one way of approaching a task. Adaptive experts are skilled in all of these different modes. They see merit in each of them. Specifically they are comfortable moving between the two more reflective modes (theorising and reflecting) and the two more associated with action (activist and pragmatist). This combination of reflection in action is an extremely powerful one.

Communities of practice

In terms of the patterns of social interaction that are most likely to foster adaptive intelligence there is compelling evidence to suggest that, in all aspects of our lives, we should actively become involved with groups of people who share our interests in such a way that we maximise our potential for learning.

I realise that this sounds both prescriptive and controlling – "Why should I structure my social life at all?" "How dare you tell me who I should hang out with!" – but just hear me out! So much of what I have been writing about is based on the assumption that learning is something done by individuals and largely taught.

But according to researchers Jean Lave and Etienne Wenger, real learning takes place in a "community of practice". Communities of practice are everywhere in our lives. We may call them sports clubs or teams, reading or walking groups, churches or mosques – any community of people engaged in an activity with a shared purpose.

Sometimes we are core members; sometimes we are at the edge of the group. In our real-life learning we are constantly engaged in a range of activities whether largely to pay our bills, for pleasure or both. The characteristics of these communities of practice vary considerably. Some are formal, others are more fluid. But there is a level of engagement in a joint enterprise and a shared repertoire of routines, approaches, techniques and skills that the members of the community have developed over a period of time. Communities of practice are also bound together by a set of relationships.

In a community of practice you learn through participation in a complex, self-organising system. The learning you acquire is very much part of the cooperative social relationships that bind the group together. These provide the effective context for learning to thrive. Much of Lave and Wenger's thinking derives from their observation of apprentices at work. They conclude that, to begin with, people have to join communities and learn "at the periphery". Then, as they become more competent, they move more to the "centre" of a particular community. Learning is much more a social journey as part of the learner's participation in any group than the specific acquisition of knowledge or skills by individuals.

We learn by doing but the doing is very much situated in a particular community. The simple message from all of Lave and Wenger's work is the desirability of getting involved with a range of different groups. In some ways there is nothing radically different about this approach. It simply affirms what many of us know intuitively: that informal learning is a largely social process.

The interesting issue raised by the community of practice idea is the degree to which you progress from the periphery of a group (where those who are less expert reside) to being closer to its centre (where those with accumulated expertise and wisdom are). In an effective group, those who are more confident, and probably more skilled, see it as their responsibility not just to welcome new members but also to act to offer them advice.

Rule 5 – The argument so far

At the core of what it takes to thrive in a period of accelerated change is adaptive intelligence. This involves a blend of imitating, experimenting, creative problem-solving and reflection in action. In terms of social interaction, valuable learning experiences can be derived from active participation in communities of practice, from one-to-one coaching and from action learning sets.

Last words:

> Keep on the lookout for novel ideas that others have used
> successfully. Your idea has to be original only in its adap-
> tation to the problem you're working on.

Thomas Edison

Rule 6 – No one can make you change

Human freedom is not an illusion; it is an objective phenomenon, distinct from all other biological conditions and found in only one species, us.

Daniel Dennett

It's a free world

The world is moved along, not only by the mighty shoves of its heroes, but also by the aggregate of the tiny pushes of each honest worker.

Helen Keller

While we often talk of living in a free world and exercising free will, in reality many of us think that we are powerless to resist change. Things happen on the global stage and we assume that we are just mere bit-players in the unfolding drama. The latest credit crunch, the remorseless march of technology, rising retirement ages, cheap flights, the latest set of organisational priorities – whatever the issue, it is all too easy simply to get swept up by it and see little opportunity for individual free will and personal impact.

In fact, the view of the world that says that it is impossible for a small number of people to have any impact on big issues is wrong on two counts. First, it is simply not true that big issues or ideas leave no room for individual dissent. Think no further than the very slow acceptance of, say, the science of climate change and the large number of people who live as if it were not happening. Or, at a personal level, despite overwhelming evidence of the damage done to us by smoking or the harmful effects of obesity, ponder why it is that so many people still choose to smoke and why our diets get less not more healthy. We are surrounded by examples of significant numbers of individuals moving against the direction of travel with regard to new thinking which has changed our understanding of something.

By the same token, despite the steadily increasing global population, individuals and small groups of "honest workers" are still able significantly to influence the way things happen. The World Wide Web started with a very small number of people. The phenomenon that is J. K. Rowling and Harry Potter was largely created through the word of mouth of, initially, a small number of children in the UK. Indeed with the advent of blogging individual writers are exerting this kind of power every day.

Whether you do or do not see a real role for yourself as having the capacity to influence what goes on around you will depend to a large extent on how you account for what happens as you go through life. In Rule 2 we looked at Julian Rotter's powerful idea of our locus of control, the degree to which we ascribe the causality of events to things within or beyond our control. And in Rule 4 we explored Martin Seligman's idea of "explanatory style", the degree to which we see things that happen to us as permanent, somehow personalised (i.e. happening to us in some unfair way) or pervasive to our lives (where something going wrong in one area infects our view of everything else).

The result of a pessimistic view of the world is almost certainly likely to be a set of limiting beliefs about our role within it, just as a locus of control sees what happens to us as being essentially beyond our influence. It is all too easy to start an inner voice in our head which constantly undermines our determination and hope.

The risk of exposing yourself

Notwithstanding what I have just said about the power of individuals to resist change and the idea that we are essentially powerless to resist the inexorable force of change, there is some truth in the inevitability of our personal views being overcome.

Look at this piece of wallpaper for a moment. With its distinctive patterns it will immediately take some of us back to the 1960s. Were you to discover something like it on the wall of a new house or flat your reaction might be something along the lines of "that dreadful wallpaper has to go". Now imagine you have settled into your new home and some months have elapsed.

One evening you are sitting with your family and you find a little voice in the back of your head saying to you: "that wallpaper's beginning to grow on me". If this happens you will have experienced the "mere exposure effect". This powerful piece of human behaviour, discovered by Robert Zajonc, found that the more you show people something the more they tend to like it. It describes the way that, simply by experiencing something we tend to become more warmly predisposed to it. (By the way, if 1960s wallpaper is something you really like in a retro sort of way, then substitute your own taste nightmare instead to get the full value from this example: swirly Artex ceilings, leaded glass windows and so on.) Familiarity breeds not contempt but content!

Knowing about this effect is enormously helpful for anyone experiencing change. Experience, as the old adage has it, is the best teacher. But exposure to experience comes with a price tag! It may just get under our skin. Good leaders know this and use it to their advantage by constantly providing opportunities for their people to experiment with new ideas in a safe environment.

Of course the mere exposure effect can be exploited and abused. Leaders of change could, in theory, calculate that simply by forcing people to be exposed to a new way of doing things, they will change their minds. But simply providing the opportunity to experience things rarely does the trick. You need also to create a culture in which experimentation and risk-taking is accepted and encouraged. And there is always the chance – featured in this Rule – that people may not go along with you.

From the individual's perspective, knowing how exposure to new ideas tends to make us disposed to them is a useful safeguard against being too easily impressed in the face of novelty. Experience really does matter. Or, as Will Rogers amusingly suggests: "There are three kinds of men, ones that learn by reading, a few who learn by observation, and the rest of them have to pee on the electric fence and find out for themselves."

In fact good ideas – "memes" as Richard Dawkins calls them – are transmitted more like a viral infection than through more mechanistic processes. This is the tipping point image of an epidemic introduced by Malcolm Gladwell that we met in Rule 4. Ideas gather momentum then, like a see-saw which has been more or less balanced, suddenly gain momentum and take off.

Albert Bandura's work is interesting with regard to vicarious experience. It turns out that even experience at one remove has its value in making us more responsive to change. In a series of experiments with people who were terrified of snakes, Bandura showed that simply by safely watching from behind glass doors, while others handled the snakes without any signs of distress, phobics could gain sufficient confidence first to walk into the room and simply look at a snake safely contained inside a glass tank, then gradually to actually touch and hold one. It seems that one of the things going on in this situation is a recalculation by the phobic about their preconceived fears about likely results from, in this case, handling a snake. However much you had told someone afraid of snakes to trust you and try handling them, it is highly unlikely that this would have worked. Creating a situation in which, even vicariously, they can experience a result which differs from their previous imagined thoughts can be a powerful force for change.

Modern day alchemy

Two themes run through this Rule, the power of individuals to exercise free will (and resist change) and create compelling change. Management guru Charles Handy has recently explored this idea by creating a gallery of influential people who have used their individual power to move mountains. In *The New Alchemists* he takes the powerful myth of turning base metal into gold and gives it a contemporary spin. For the individuals he identifies have, in a sense, made gold out of base ingredients by exerting their own personal alchemy. Handy selects twenty-nine individuals from the UK who demonstrate these special powers.

From this group, five individuals illustrate the breadth of his selection:

- Sir William Atkinson who took on a large London failing secondary school which no one else would touch and turned it round. This became the aptly named Phoenix School.

- Trevor Baylis, a serial inventor, who created the wind-up radio and a range of other products aimed especially at Africa where the creation of clockwork equipment provides sufficient power in parts of the continent where electricity is scarce.

- Andy Law, founder of a radical advertising agency St Lukes, which was the first of its kind to be collectively owned and democratically led by its employees, and which turned its own offices into extraordinarily innovative spaces.

- Julia Middleton, creator of Common Purpose, an organisation devoted to bringing emerging leaders together for real-world learning opportunities in organisations which they would not normally experience, frequently in other sectors.

- Jane Tewson, inventor of Comic Relief, whose persistence and creativity created the world's most effective use of comedy to raise funds for charitable work.

Through interviews with these "alchemists" and by looking at earlier analyses of highly successful people, Handy concludes that they share three habits of mind.

1. Dedication – each, in different ways, is a driven person.

2. Doggedness – each is determinedly persistent and resourceful.

3. Difference – each sees difference as a badge of honour.

Handy reflects that the three qualities of mind he identifies are not far from those identified by Francis Galton (Charles Darwin's cousin). Galton suggested that the three ingredients of genius are ability, zeal and a capacity for hard work.

Returning, for a moment, to Malcolm Gladwell's analysis of the way in which ideas are like epidemics, in *The Tipping Point*, it is worth dwelling on one of the conclusions he draws. He calls it the "Law of the Few" and cites a number of contemporary examples of people who have single-handedly influenced events. He explores in particular the extraordinary impact of Paul Revere's midnight ride in 1775 from Boston to Lexington at the start of the American War of Independence as an example of how one man can mobilise many others. Gladwell argues that it only takes a few people to create a sea change, especially if they are what he calls "connectors" or "mavens" – gregarious individuals who are plugged into a variety of social networks.

At the same time, in *Living on Thin Air,* Charles Leadbeater was making a similar point about the ways in which knowledge is created, as it were, alchemically. Leadbeater talks specifically about the need to balance exploitation of existing ideas with the creation of new ones. Sometimes they get this wrong and lose out in the evolutionary battle for survival, as with Xerox (which was slow to deal with the threat to its profits from cheap copies from Japanese machines) or Kodak (which took time to find a replacement for its reproduction of photographs in an age of digital cameras). The company 3M is often cited as being a model of an effective adaptive, innovative organisation and it has a 70:30 rule, with a goal of 30 per cent of income coming from new ideas and 70 per cent from existing products and services.

As the Rule began by asserting, it's a free world. With modern technological advances, far from being more likely to be caught up with the flow, individuals actually have a power to speak and influence like they never have before. No one can make us change but to thrive we may often choose to do just that. And as we navigate our way through complex times certain approaches may be more helpful than others.

Self-understanding

While resistance to change can be a strength (as we will see in more detail in the next Rule) simply resisting for resistance's sake is clearly not a helpful behaviour. This is where an individual's degree of self-understanding comes in. We need to know enough about ourselves to know whether, for example, we are demonstrating useful doggedness or irksome and cussed stubbornness. We need to learn when it is better to keep niggling away at a problem and when we would be better to put it to one side and get on with something else.

A real understanding of self is specifically helpful when it comes to understanding the way we go about our learning. I am not here referring to the idea of learning styles, interesting as they are, which we encountered in Rule 5 and which have become a very effective meme in organisational life today.

Robert Sternberg and Richard Wagner put it well when they write: "Intelligence boils down to your ability to know your strengths and weaknesses and to capitalise on the strengths while compensating for the weaknesses."

As we go through life we get better at spotting those situations in which we learn effectively and those in which we fare less well. That's one aspect of our adaptive intelligence at work. So, for example, we begin to realise that there are certain frames of mind in which we are more or less creative, specific times of day when we do our best thinking work – a time in the evening after which we are capable of little more than watching television or, in some people's cases, the night owls, come alive and relish the challenge of a new creative task. We discover how and in what situations we are able to receive and act upon feedback from others without becoming overly defensive. Or we realise when we consciously need to use certain mind tools to approach certain tasks if we are to be able to accomplish them effectively; a list works well for shopping but may be less helpful if we are musing on a problem and trying to see how elements of it connect together, in which case we may prefer to use a mind map or other less linear approach.

This kind of self-awareness will help us to get better at recognising when our resistance to change is a potentially useful check and balance allowing us time to investigate more or when it masks our own unhelpful and sometimes defensive reactions to new experience.

Tool – Knowing you

Use this reflective process to help you take stock of how you do in different situations. Which do you do well in? Which cause you anxiety? Which do you find difficult?

Think back over the last month. Call to mind anything new or different or challenging that has happened to you. Which did you do well at? Which did you find more difficult?

And when you have made two lists, ponder what your lists tell you about you and about the kind of change situations you find easy and those which challenge you. Why do you think this is? Are there any patterns? What could you do differently?

Do well   *Find difficult*

Goal-setting

An important component for anyone deciding what to assimilate into their life and what to reject is the degree to which we are able to set and use goals. We touched on this briefly when discussing Lev Vygotsky's idea of proximal development, the idea that we all have a "growth" zone outside our present comfort one.

Two people's research into goal-setting and motivation has largely shaped our understanding today, Edwin Locke and Gary Latham. In the 1960s first Locke and then Latham argued that employees were motivated by clear goals and appropriate feedback and that simply working towards a goal was a major source of motivation to actually reaching the goal, which, in turn, improved performance. Indeed specific and difficult goals result in better performance on tasks than vague or easy goals.

A general request to someone to "try harder" is much less effective than "try to increase your speed by one item per twenty minutes". Hard goals are more motivating than easy goals, because it's much more of an accomplishment to achieve something that you have to work for.

In 1990, in *A Theory of Goal Setting and Task Performance*, Locke and Latham concluded their analysis of goal-setting by suggesting five principles. Goals, they argue, are effective according to the degree to which they contain one of the following five things:

1. Clarity – effective goals are unambiguous and measurable.

2. Challenge – we are motivated by achievement and respond well to challenge.

3. Commitment – if a goal is understood and agreed to, ideally willingly, there is likely to be more buy-in.

4. Feedback – regular feedback and opportunities to measure progress are important.

5. Complexity of task – the more complex a task, the more it needs to be clearly broken down into achievable elements.

From this research the now widely used acronym SMART was derived. SMART exists in a number of different forms of which these are the main ones:

S – smart
M – measurable
A – attainable, achievable, actionable
R – relevant, realistic
T – timely

Tool – Setting SMART goals

Think of something in your life that you want to do, not do or change.

Use the SMART framework to write down an achievable goal to help you make progress.

If we are to make progress and evolve, then goals are crucial ways of ensuring that we avoid getting blown off course. And if we know these simple but effective principles of effective goal-setting, then we are more likely to achieve what we want to do. There is an important relationship, too, with Carol Dweck's thinking about growth mindsets in the sense that we should not underestimate the desirability of setting ourselves stretching challenges. Far from being off-putting, if well calibrated these can nurture a growth mindset, for the sense of achievement is likely to be far greater the harder the task and the level of motivation, if often correspondingly higher.

Open-mindedness

A core attribute when it comes to dealing with change effectively is the degree to which we can remain open to experience without feeling forced to decide one way or the other. Indeed in some ways, as John Paul Getty said, "in times of rapid change, experience could be your worst enemy". For if our assumption is that we have "been here before" we may draw from a limited palette of experiences whenever we deal with change.

Ellen Langer has defined a certain kind of open-mindedness which she calls "mindfulness". This involves the ability to be constantly creating new categories, an openness to new information or data or experiences and an assumption that, in most situations, there will be more than one perspective.

Mindfulness can in many ways be seen at its most natural in the young child who is constantly remaking, creating, trying out new things and exploring other points of view. It often involves a high degree of playfulness. In Rule 3 I referred to Langer's experiment in which she demonstrated how tasks are achieved more effectively if done playfully. Perhaps not surprisingly adults find it hard to maintain playfulness as they grow older. It is too easily seen as juvenile or childish behaviour when often it can be exactly what is required to lead to a breakthrough in thinking. You may also want to refer to the section on "being" in Rule 3 which has something in common with this.

A major obstacle to our development is the opposite of Langer's mindfulness – mindlessness. We have known for many years how unhelpful this can be. Here's Francis Bacon: "Human understanding when it has once adopted an opinion … draws all things else to support and agree with it." And John Stuart Mill was clear about the importance of keeping the mind open to criticism of opinions and conduct; we need to be able to continue to imagine alternatives, to be open-minded for as long as possible. Unless that it is we are in a fast-sinking boat or a war zone in which prompt action is, of course, the order of the day!

Courage

The capacity to be courageous is an enduringly human one. It is the disposition, voluntarily, to take altruistic action which may carry personal risk to ensure the achievement of a greater good for an individual or for a group. The notion of courage introduces an all-important moral dimension into any discussion of evolution and change. Plato distinguished between discerning courage and rash bravery in his *Dialogues* where he has Socrates making this distinction. For him the critical difference between these two aspects of courageous behaviour is the degree of forethought involved.

Not surprisingly most of the thinking about courage has used warfare as the source of its evidence. The emphasis has therefore been on physical bravery. However, with the advent of psychology many have shown how a rudimentary distinction between physical and moral bravery is too crude. Both involve an individual dealing with their fears and in many situations no such pure difference can be drawn.

Christopher Peterson and Martin Seligman's excellent handbook on *Character Strengths and Virtues* helpfully defines courage as having three other components along with bravery – persistence, integrity and vitality. Each of these traits is associated with certain useful habits of mind in terms of successful adaptation.

While a dog may gnaw away at a bone for a long time it is not showing persistence in the sense that we use it to describe long-term activity in spite of potential obstacles. The dog may worry away at its bone off and on for a long while, but it is simply motivated by the taste and smell of the bone and its marrow or the physical jaw strengthening it instinctively enjoys. You only have to imagine any pioneer civilization to see how enormous levels of persistence in the face of adverse weather and uncertain resources must have been essential to survival.

In this Rule we have been celebrating individual perseverance and the fact that it can and does contribute to our evolution as a species. At the same time we have suggested that it is not sensible to resist change for the sake of it. This is where people who are doggedly persistent can be their own worst enemy. In some cases, for example when we have become stale and over-tired as we try to complete a project against a tight deadline, we need to stop persisting and take a break. It is easy to conjecture how the capacity to keep going was developed by our ancestors as only some of them managed to keep going for long enough to find a fresh source of food and establish a new camp. It has consequently been inherited by us all. You can see its extreme form in round-the-world sailors or in mountaineers. The former group in particular, especially when going solo, have demonstrated how high levels of performance can be maintained on minimal sleep (often as little as five hours a day divided into three or four catnaps). For most of us mere mortals, while our minds and bodies may be capable theoretically of such feats, the toll it would take on our well-being and health would be enormous.

There are two particular benefits of persistence in terms of our ongoing ability to adapt. The first is the relatively obvious one that, by keeping going and overcoming obstacles we learn and become expert in new mind tools which we can then apply in other aspects of our lives. So someone who persists with a relationship with a loved one over a long period may acquire increased self-understanding and be able to operate with higher levels of emotional intelligence as a consequence.

The second benefit is the fact that we tend to enjoy our success even more if we have had to stick at it against the odds. Most of us have had a glimpse of this experience. Perhaps, as a non-hillwalker, we have made it to the top of a mountain with a group of friends or, despite our nerves, we have managed to give a short speech at a family wedding.

An important idea related to this second area is cognitive dissonance, first developed by Leon Festinger fifty years ago. Cognitive dissonance is the psychological discomfort we feel when our actions conflict with our beliefs or when we offer opinions, perhaps under pressure from others, with which we do not agree.

According to this theory, individuals tend to seek consistency among their beliefs and opinions. When there is a gap between our attitudes or behaviours something has to shift to remove the dissonance. Dissonant situations are things like this:

I like chocolate. I am trying to lose weight.

I smoke. I am a healthy person who enjoys taking exercise.

I believe everyone can develop and grow. I work in a school where children are grouped into able, average and slow learners.

We have three clear options when dealing with any dissonance we encounter in our lives:

1. We can reduce the importance of any dissonant beliefs ("But a few pieces of chocolate won't make much difference").

2. We can add more beliefs with which we are comfortable that outweigh the dissonant beliefs ("But generally I have a healthy diet and exercise a lot").

3. We can change the dissonant beliefs so that they are no longer inconsistent ("Actually I am happy with my weight and shape").

Dissonance occurs most often when we have to choose between two incompatible beliefs or actions. It is particularly difficult when two alternative courses of action are equally attractive!

Part of the reason explaining why we may or may not choose to change any course of action could be to do with the tension induced by cognitive dissonance. Persuasive orators (and politicians) know this. They deliberately exaggerate a sense of dissonance between the status quo and the actions they would like us to follow.

A fascinating example of the theory of cognitive dissonance being put into practice is the case of the Pink Pistols, a gay-friendly shooting club started by Doug Krick in the US. The two beliefs would seem to be: (1) gun-owners are macho men who hate gay men and (2) gay men are against the use of macho things like guns. The Pink Pistols challenge the stereotype about what gay people do or do not do and challenge common views of gay people at the same time. As a result it becomes difficult to think of gun owners as homophobic when confronted with the reality of a shooting club aimed at and run by sexual minorities. Many have to reconsider their beliefs about gun ownership.

That we like our beliefs and actions to be consonant is a powerful force in determining whether we change our actions and/or change our beliefs. Given its potency it perhaps helps to account for why we feel particularly pleased when, through sheer persistence, we change the way we do something in order to align our thoughts and actions.

Associated with this kind of consonant behaviour is the idea of integrity. A combination of authentic and honest behaviour, we act with most integrity when we are truest to ourselves – when our private and public selves are in harmony. Although these ideas have been around for half a millennium, it was the humanistic psychologists of the 1960s who gave it particular expression, with Carl Rogers preeminent among these. The idea of "congruence" developed by Rogers is close to integrity and has provided fuel for the client-centred therapy movement ever since. Essentially this involves skilled therapists helping their clients to get in touch with their real feelings so that they can bring their lives into greater balance. This is a particularly complex area as we will sometimes choose to maintain a persona which is different from what we really think and feel. In evolutionary terms there are clear benefits to the species in developing integrity or congruence. First, at an individual level, if we can accurately read our inner feelings we are much more likely to be a fully functioning member of the human race. Second, in the broader social context, it is much easier to get along with people who mean what they say and say what they mean. Collaborative activity becomes much more productive. And third, as we saw in Rule 2, people who are able to deal with their inner feelings and "move on" from them find it easier to deal with change.

Chris Arygris has a useful concept here. He talks of "theory in use" and "espoused theory". Our theory in use is what we actually do, while our espoused theory is what we profess to believe. If there is too much of a gap between the two, it can be difficult to build relationships which have integrity. Given the choice, most of us tend to judge people by what they do, not what they say they do!

Quite apart from any theories about why we do or do not choose to change, there is the built-in biology of it all. However sensible an idea might be, we become attached to our own ways of doing things and, the older we grow, the deeper these attachments become.

Helpful patterns of social interaction

The actions of individuals matter but no one can force an individual to do something that is against their will. It follows from this that the more social situations we can put ourselves in which will give us opportunities to explore any tensions inherent in these propositions the better. A really fruitful example of just such a milieu is "action learning".

Invented by Reg Revans in the 1980s, action learning is becoming increasingly popular with organisations, but the approach it suggests is also highly relevant for us in our private lives. Action learning is a process of enquiry. It starts with the identification of a real problem or issue. A group then comes together to find solutions through a process of enquiry. Typically, this is how it works: a small group of individuals, often from different organisations and possibly with different professional backgrounds, come together for the specific purpose of learning together. Sometimes one person acts a facilitator.

The group establishes a trusting and confidential atmosphere in which it is safe to share difficult issues. Individuals take it in turn to describe one or more real business or organisational issues with which they are currently struggling. The group then decides which of these they would like to tackle. In some cases the combined group expertise will be enough to provide useful answers to individual issues but often a process of collaborative enquiry is called for – normally action learning that lasts over a period of months.

In such a situation various kinds of useful interactions can take place. Fundamentally it is a place where you can think out loud, working your way through complex situations, often dissonant ones where either your own or someone else's behaviours are not seeming quite right. Faced with a possible change of direction, you can use an action learning set to help you figure out whether the stance you are adopting so far is a sensible or coherent one, or whether you are possibly resisting for resisting's sake.

Exactly in the spirit of this Rule an action learning set provides an arena where advice, if sought, can be given but where it is absolutely clear that it is up to you whether you choose to accept it or act upon it. The language used in sessions like this needs to be carefully chosen. So, for example, if advice is given it tends to be most helpful to offer it in the form of "You might like to" rather than "You ought to". The former offers the recipient the unambiguous option of rejecting any advice which they find unhelpful or are not ready for. It is also very practical.

> "Why," said the Dodo, "the best way to explain it is to do it."
>
> Lewis Carroll, *Alice in Wonderland*

Rule 6 – The argument so far

Even though there may frequently be great pressure put on us, no one can make you change. As individuals of courage we can choose to act differently from the herd; indeed there are many good examples of when this can be helpful. Certain habits of mind seem to be particularly associated with the maintenance of appropriate determination to act differently and make a difference, including self-understanding, goal-setting, open-mindedness and courage. In the next Rule we will go a stage further and explore the situations in which resistance is necessary if you are to be true to yourself.

Last words:

> Never doubt that a small group of thoughtful committed citizens can change the world. Indeed it's the only thing that ever has.
>
> Margaret Mead

Rule 7 – Sometimes it's smart to resist

Only the wisest and stupidest of men never change.

Confucius

The algebra of change

> Reasonable people adapt themselves to the world. Unreasonable people attempt to adapt the world to themselves. All progress, therefore, depends on unreasonable people.
>
> George Bernard Shaw

It's easy to get cast as a Luddite if you resist change. Indeed the pressure to come into line, especially in the corporate arena, is intense. Within an organisation, to resist the latest change of direction from the leadership is likely to cost you your job.

In fact the degree to which the Luddites were anti-technology (the new wide looms which threatened skilled jobs) or part of a more complex protest against the sudden introduction of a free market is a contested subject. When George Bernard Shaw talks of change being dependent on unreasonable people he is right in two respects. You have to persuade the unreasonable (or "laggards" to use the language of Everett Rogers) to join in if you are trying to change people's minds. But, given that we sometimes get it wrong first time, the unreasonable person often ends up by being the reasonable one in the long run.

Much of *rEvolution* so far has been taken up with arguing that adaptation is essentially necessary and inevitable. But in this Rule I want to make the case for apparently unreasonable opposition to new ideas. Interestingly even the word "unreasonable" is a loaded one, with its Enlightenment overtones (of rationality and reason being the only smart response to the world).

I suspect that sometimes change is judged too much on intellectual and rational grounds and that, even if the affective domain is considered, it counts for less. Grounds for divorce in the UK interestingly include unreasonable (but not unemotional) behaviour!

To make my case I am going to adopt a different, more personal tone in this Rule. My argument goes like this: I believe that I have a good track record of adaptive behaviour. A reasonable person looking at my curriculum vitae and personal story so far would be hard pressed to disagree with this assessment. In all areas of my life I actively embrace change.

Earlier I touched on issues of personality and change, so it might just be helpful for anyone interested in the Myers-Briggs Type Indicator, that on this particular psychometric I rate myself as ENFP (Extravert, iNtuitive, Feeler, Perceiver). This may suggest certain preferences for involvement, action and flexibility with lots of options and open-ended plans.

Despite being temperamentally and by personality "type" very open to change, I am passionately opposed to a number of the trends that I see today. Am I a Luddite? Or am I right to resist? You, gentle reader, will be the judge of this, as I focus on just two areas of my life. Both of them have something to do with how I choose to spend my time.

My first concern centres on the impact of scientific progress on my home. In the last few decades there have been enormous advances. I can buy all the food I need online. I can buy it pre-prepared and put it in a clever oven with a complex time-setting to cook it so that it is ready for me just when I want it. (If I had a very smart home I could even access all the machines remotely from a hand-held device kept in my pocket so that I could turn things on or off and adjust timings to suit changes in my plans.) Or, of course, I can use the microwave oven and speed up the whole process so that I do not waste time.

I can then eat while watching something either on my television or on a screen of some kind attached to a computer's memory. I am no longer tied to TV schedules because I can either subscribe to a provider who allows me to watch content whenever I want to, or I can download public service broadcasts from the BBC for free up to a week after they have been broadcast. Once I have finished my TV dinner I can then migrate to incredibly sophisticated computer games, don a pair of headphones, connect to the World Wide Web and lose myself for hours in clever competitive games, often involving "killing" my fellow human beings. What incredible evolutionary progress! What wonderful scientific and technological invention has been shown here. Or is it?

Of course it isn't. I only have so much discretionary time in my life – the minutes, days and hours when I actively choose to do something – and these inventions either deprive me, by being too easily available, of all-important time to develop my interests or be with my family and friends (the smart television) or go too fast (the prepared meal) and so prevent me from slowing down and enjoying mealtime reflective conversations.

My second issue touches on the toxicity of many parenting and childhood practices. Recently Sue Palmer has explored this issue very fully in her excellent book, *Toxic Childhood: How the Modern World Is Damaging Our Children and What We Can Do About It*. My concerns are about the systematic removal of risk in childhood and, perhaps surprisingly, the overuse of praise by parents.

The scene I painted of evenings dominated by the television screen and the soulless eating of junk food are bad enough for adults, but what if they are applied to children? What if this kind of social interaction is the norm as they grow up? The bad news, of course, is that it is. And the situation is compounded by another change – the tendency for two parents or carers to be working. This means that many children come home from school and face an unsupervised period of a couple of hours before an adult is on the scene again. Television soap adults and morality free computer games have effectively become parents to a generation of children.

There are at least two interpretations of this increasingly common arrangement. The first runs like this: children are perfectly capable of looking after themselves and, indeed, evolutionarily speaking, learn to be more autonomous and better able to survive. The other reaches a different conclusion. While in evolutionary terms it is wonderful that so many more female members of the species can undertake fulfilling paid work, the result is that their children learn certain passive habits of mind in the home which are deeply unhelpful in terms of cultivating their curiosity. Mine, you may not be surprised to know, is the second of these two views.

And it is worse still. For coupled with periods of missed opportunity these same children have virtually ceased outdoor adventurous play. For the same parents who find it acceptable to leave young children unsupervised in the home undergo a strange transformation when they come to imagine what goes on outdoors. Suddenly the streets are paved with child molesters, and trees, lanes, fields and play-grounds become unsafe spaces. The net result of this is the denial of the development of just those habits of mind – pre-tending, imagining, waiting, watching, thinking, rethink-ing – which children need to acquire if they are to become successful adapters in later life. We even feel the need to transport our children to school in the car rather than let them walk to school as they always used to. No wonder we are suffering from a global epidemic of obesity of body and, arguably, of mind. This is progress of the wrong sort; a per-vasive shift in the way we organise our lives which I believe we would be right to resist.

Sue Palmer quotes lines from Robert Louis Stevenson which beautifully capture the power of playful minds:

> Happy hearts and happy faces,
> Happy play in grassy places –
> That was how in ancient ages,
> Children grew to kings and sages.

Allied to screen-dependency, a lack of real parenting at critical moments of the day and a largely irrational fear of the outdoors is an even stranger development: the tendency to over-praise children. Whether out of guilt (that we are not being more effective, present and available parents) or a genuine wish to be positive in our relationships (a very worthwhile aspiration), parents increasingly praise their children's cleverness. But interestingly research is beginning to show us that, far from this being a useful way of building esteem, it has an unintended consequence; encouraging a child to think of him or herself as smart or clever does not help them and is more likely to hinder their progress.

In an article in *New York Magazine*, Po Bronson and Ashley Merryman cite a survey undertaken by Columbia University which says that 85 per cent of American parents believe that it is important to tell their children that they are smart. But we know (see Rule 4 where we first met Carol Dweck's research in this area) that people who have been encouraged to think of themselves as smart (through regular praise, for example) consistently underestimate their abilities and regularly shun difficult tasks (where they may fail). Children who see themselves as clever are likely to deduce that when they do well it is because they are clever rather than as result of the effort they have put in. By over-praising children we run the risk of reducing the value they put on effort.

That we have reached this situation is partly the result of the effectiveness of the "self-esteem movement". And they had a point. Children being seen and not heard, or even publicly shamed for not knowing things in class, was clearly unhelpful. Seeing the self-esteem of children as something worth nurturing is a good idea. But not if it is achieved at the expense of the all-important growth mindset which all human beings need to have if we are to adapt and change successfully.

Understanding resistance to change

Let me deal now more explicitly with the title of this Rule, the idea that there is some complex mathematics at work in figuring out a course of action when faced with a changed situation. The factors governing this process have been helpfully reduced to a formula by David Gleicher:

$$D \times V \times F > R$$

D = Dissatisfaction with how things are
V = Vision of what is possible
F = First, concrete steps that can be taken towards the vision
R = Resistance

To decide to change we tend to take into account our dissatisfaction with the status quo and set this alongside a calculation of the likelihood of us being able to do something about it. Being able to do something involves having a vision of what this might be, along with some of the practical first steps which could be taken. If all of these three components – D, V and F – add up to being more than your resistance to the new situation then you are likely to have reached the necessary tipping point to act.

In terms of any decision which we may want to take this formula gives us two areas on which we may want to focus our analytical thinking. We will want to understand just how dissatisfied we are with the current state of things. Is it really that bad? Have I talked to other people in similar situations? What's the worst thing about my current situation? What's my evidence for thinking what I do about where I am now?

And we will want to probe any potential alternatives. Do we really have a big picture of what we want to do? If so, is it plausible? As well as the "vision thing", is there a reasonable likelihood that we can achieve what we want? What exactly would this involve us doing and are there any first steps we might take that are likely to work?

Essentially, evolutionarily speaking, we need to know whether the "fire" will be any better than the "frying pan" in which we are getting "sizzled"! Then we can decide whether it is, indeed, smart or dumb to resist the change being suggested or contemplated.

If you are pro a potential change then Gleicher's formula has two very clear messages: (1) exaggerate what you are dissatisfied with and (2) make sure you have both a compelling vision and a practical implementation plan to go with it.

Of course, both of these approaches carry risks – exaggerate things too much and no one will believe you. This first tactic, sometimes known as "creating a burning platform" can also invite scepticism if the platform turns out to be burning rather slowly and weakly! In the workplace it can also cause considerable stress to people who fear for their jobs. The heat, as it were, becomes just too intense for rational responses. People begin to fear for their survival.

In terms of the second message, leaders and managers in the workplace frequently adopt one or other of these approaches (vision or first practical steps) but rarely both. So you find charismatic, persuasive people who paint a picture of the promised land but leave the fact that it will involve crossing the Red Sea as a vague detail. Or plan so well and so practically for all the vicissitudes of the "journey" that when Pharaoh's armies are hot on your heels and morale is low, fail to come up with a sufficient motivating vision to keep you all going through difficult times.

Moreover, knowing Gleicher's approach helps us whether we are the recipient or the driver of new thinking and change! Such knowledge can be powerful.

The (sometimes) stupidity of the crowd

There are other good reasons why it is sometimes smart to resist, of which the most obvious is that people are not always as wise as they like to think they are.

Humans are in many ways still pack animals. If one member of the pack seems to have found something useful, then the rest of us want to muscle in on the action. All too easily we can end up joining someone foolish who just

happens to be looking up at an empty sky. Even a small number of people pretending to stand in a queue can sometimes be enough to persuade us to go and stand in line with them on the off chance.

What we are experiencing here is a kind of social proof. Psychologists and sociologists call it "groupthink". First coined by William Whyte in the 1950s, groupthink describes the phenomenon that occurs when a group of closely-knit people value unanimity over more rigorous critical evaluation which may involve dissent and disagreement. In such situations bad decisions can easily be taken. Most of us will at some stage of our life have been in situations where an element of groupthink is involved, whether in families, in teams at work or in our wider social life. Often in hindsight we look back and wonder how we ever decided on a particular course of action until we remember the other social components of the process which perhaps led us to keeping our mouth shut rather than airing our doubts.

Research psychologist Irvin Janis has usefully identified a number of strategies which can be used to avoid descending into groupthink. These include:

1. Having someone with a critical evaluator role who freely airs doubts;

2. Ensuring that those with more power keep their counsel in the early stages of discussion;

3. Having more than one group working on any problem;

4. Using trusted outsiders and subject experts as critical friends; and

5. Ensuring that the role of devil's advocate is played at key moments in the process, consciously looking at issues from the opposite perspective.

We are more likely to fall prey to groupthink when we are with people who are very much like ourselves. (Guess who most people like to spend their time with? People like themselves. What does this mean for many of the decisions we take in our lives, you may wonder?)

This tendency to drift into conformity was famously and dramatically challenged in Sidney Lumet's classic 1957 film, *Twelve Angry Men*, where one dissenting juror, Mr Davis (played by Henry Fonda), slowly manages to convince his colleagues that the case is not as obviously clear-cut as it seemed in the courtroom and that the accused Hispanic boy may not in fact be guilty of the murder. Here is a perfect example of a situation in which it is smart to resist.

Peer pressure is a kind of groupthink, where gangs, clubs – cults even – systematise their way of doing and being such that it is all too easy to find yourself developing a kind of mindlessness where you just go along with the crowd. This effect can have an even more perverse consequence on the way we take decisions. Jerry Harvey first coined the expression "the Abilene Paradox" in an article on management practices in the 1970s. He describes a situation in which a group of people collectively decide on a course of action that none of the individual members in the group actually want to adopt. This is the Abilene Paradox, so called after Abilene, in Texas. Harvey imagines a family group who end up taking a long hot drive fifty miles or so north. Through a series of misunderstandings and wrong assumptions each person in a family group assumes that others want to embark on the drive and so they end up having a thoroughly unsatisfactory excursion! My suspicion is that this may be something that families are particularly prone to!

If power and authority are involved in pressing for a course of action it is even more important for us to be on our guard against groupthink. In a series of experiments Stanley Milgram showed just how far human beings will go without resisting if a source of authority is involved. In one now infamous experiment, Milgram pretends to conduct a test of the impact of punishment on memory and learning. The test involves learning a list of paired words until they are perfectly memorised. The subject's role in the experiment is to test another subject (in fact an actor who is part of the research team) and administer electric shocks if the learner makes a mistake. The experiment supervisor is suitably dressed in a white lab coat which clearly confers a sense of authority on him. The subject is told that, although the shocks hurt, they cause no lasting damage or harm.

As the learner begins to make mistakes, so the subject turns up the dial and the shocks get worse. The actor playing the learner starts to plead with the subject not to carry on. But, and here's the shocking reality, almost none of the subjects stopped before they had completed all thirty of the different levels of shock right up to one that was, allegedly, 450 volts.

So why did subjects not stop immediately and show some humanity? Milgram's conclusion is simple: most people's inclination to obey authority is stronger than their empathy with other people's pain. If you want a compelling reason as to why it is sometimes sensible to resist people in authority who tell you to change, this is surely a good one. Even if you were simply to operate the precautionary principle, you might want to invest additional cognitive effort in dealing with instructions to change from anyone in authority. Interestingly, of course, there are many people who carry authority which might transcend the logic of any proposed change. Teachers have it (sometimes). Doctors have it to such a degree that we are often awed into submitting to the medical establishment's views. The police and military services have it. Managers and organisational leaders have it (along with considerable power including the capacity to affect your continuing employment). Parents have it to a certain extent (although hormones mean that children often have to challenge it anyway!). Some politicians have it. Even if someone does not have the authority which goes with certain positions, they can dress in such a way that they appear to be authoritative (e.g. a dark suit or uniform) or they can surround themselves with the trappings of authority (e.g. large corporate offices).

Many people, in short, notwithstanding the current fashionable interest in the wisdom of crowds, are frequently wrong. Although, at an instinctive level – the pack animal in us all – we may seek safety in numbers, we would be wise to adopt the lone wolf role from time to time, too. This applies to any fashion or accepted way of doing things. It applies to all website content created by crowds, especially Wikipedia and its ilk.

Grit in the oyster

As Shaw observes, unreasonable people attempt to adapt the world to themselves. They are so confident of their vision that they sometimes manage to turn a simple oyster into a pearl of great price. Against the odds they rethink the way we see the world, as Archimedes did bringing water uphill or Copernicus did putting the sun not the earth at the centre of the universe. Or Picasso and cubism, or Freud and the human mind, or Einstein and his determined use of theoretical physics to explain ideas that had baffled scientists for years or, in our lifetimes, Nelson Mandela and his extraordinary blend of resistance to apartheid, alongside direct action and nobility of spirit. All of these individuals were "unreasonable" people in the sense that they would not accept the prevailing world view and did something about it so that the world view then changed.

Sometimes interesting ideas can be turned into great pearls because individuals do not immediately accept them, but wrestle with them to make them better. A conscious decision not to reject something out of hand but to grapple with difficult or original thoughts before coming to a decision is a smart tactic in a situation which is changing rapidly. A number of eminent scientists have ended up strongly defending the concept of global warming, for example, partly because after their initial scepticism, and through much scientific wrestling, they have come to see its logic as frighteningly compelling.

Howard Gardner, in *Changing Minds*, talks of his own dislike of "deconstructivism", the idea that it is not possible to give a coherent or single explanation of anything and that all truth is relative. While the skilled social scientist in him rejects this, he nevertheless honestly admits: "I would be disingenuous if I did not concede that I, too, have been influenced by my own encounters with these ideas. I feel less prone to make definitive statements about what is right or wrong, I am more likely to acknowledge the importance of stance, power, influence, trendiness. I am more alert to potential contradictions."

The inevitability of mind changing

At a more fundamental level, if we do not change our minds in response to changing circumstances we are unlikely to survive as one fine day the problem we face will be so different from an earlier one that it will catch us out! A splendid organisation in the US, the Edge Foundation, established in 1988, "promotes inquiry into and discussion of intellectual, philosophical, artistic, and literary issues, as well as to work for the intellectual and social achievement of society". Every year it poses a question and then engages the best minds in the world in answering it.

Here's their question for 2008:

> *When thinking changes your mind, that's philosophy.*
> *When God changes your mind, that's faith.*
> *When facts change your mind, that's science.*

What have you changed your mind about? Why?

Science is based on evidence. What happens when the data change? How have scientific findings or arguments changed your mind?

Go to the Edge Foundation's website (www.edge.org) and you are in a powerful world of ideas. But the prevailing and most interesting aspect of these, for *rEvolution*, at least in 2008, is that they are testimonies from eminent thinkers about how they have either become more or less unreasonable. At any rate they have changed their minds in the light of external circumstances or internal reflection. Social psychologist David Myers lists many things about which he, after reading and reporting on psychological science, has changed his mind, leading to his current beliefs:

> Newborns are not the blank slates I once presumed.
> Electroconvulsive therapy often alleviates intractable depression.
> Economic growth has not improved our morale.
> The automatic unconscious mind dwarfs the controlled conscious mind.
> Traumatic experiences rarely get repressed.
> Personality is unrelated to birth order.
> Most folks have high self-esteem (which sometimes causes problems).
> Opposites do not attract.
> Sexual orientation is a natural, enduring disposition (most clearly so for men), not a choice.

His is just one example. The website however is splendid testimony to one strand of argument in this Rule. You may not agree with any of the assertions which Myers makes. That is, of course, your right as a reasonably unreasonable person!

Some "unreasonable" habits of mind

To be sure that any resistance to new thinking is a sensible strategy there are a number of mindsets which may be helpful.

Analytical thinking

Unsurprisingly to avoid being duped and to ensure you know when to resist, when to challenge, when to support and when to know you need to go away and think more about something, bringing an analytical mind to bear is always helpful. (But see also the next suggested habit below, intuitive thinking, which is also extremely useful and normally used more effectively when checked out against rational arguments.)

Earlier we looked at the idea of visible thinking and discussed the benefits of becoming more aware of your thought processes. In a sense, automatically bringing your analytical mind to bear on any new issue is simply an aspect of this. Some would argue, at least in the Western world, that it was invented by the Greeks, lost for many centuries and then rediscovered by the Enlightenment. There is some truth in this. Some problems – when conditions are static, when competing options need to be considered, when a good explanation or account is required or when there is enough time to apply analytical disciplines – respond well to analytical disciplines.

Arguably we are born with enough analytical skill to survive ("Is that a horse or a lion that I see before me?") but learn analytical approaches which are more than the binary decision: "Is this animal a friend or a threat to my survival, is it a flight or fight moment?" Indeed, analysis is, at its simplest level, the ability to break down more complex problems into their component parts, consider these, make appropriate choices and decisions and put the whole lot back together. "Should I travel by train, plane, car, bicycle or foot from Manchester to Winchester?" is the kind of question which can be analysed. Each of the potential modes of transport can be considered in isolation in terms of time taken, cost, comfort and practicality. If on a fundraising tour, then walking may win out. If going to a business meeting but keen to return to your family, then flying will appear attractive. Worried about your global footprint and you might opt for the train. Needing to stop off en route to pick up a large package then the car has it. And so on.

Analysis involves getting to the bottom line of something you are reading or watching. What's the main argument being made and how is it being presented? If I were writing a newspaper headline for it, what would this be? It also involves checking for inconsistencies and being aware of where a line of argument is flawed and when a conclusion drawn is unsound. And, of course, it requires us to consider the relative strengths or weaknesses of any evidence with which we are being presented.

A core analytical skill is the ability to winnow out the "likely to be true" from the "probably snake oil" whenever you are dealing with new information. Try this approach.[1]

Tool – Crap detecting

Here are six good questions that can be adapted for a variety of situations:

1. Is the source a recognised authority on the subject in hand?

2. Does the source have a motive other than sharing true information? (If so, what is the motive?)

3. Does the source stand to gain financially or reputationally?

4. Is the source known to be emotionally unreliable, that is of sound judgement or fanatical?

5. Is the science or opinion sound? Are there some easily accessible sources to check and verify the writer's statements? (In which case use them.)

6. Do the source's ideas chime in with your own common sense and experience?

---

[1] Adapted from *Napoleon Hill's Keys to Success: The 17 Principles of Personal Achievement* (New York: Penguin, 1994).

At some stage almost every issue needs analysis and an analytical frame of mind is therefore an essential part of what it is to be an effective survivor. However, the analytical approach works less well when there is not enough time to process information, when emotions and perspective are involved and when there are multiple components which all need to be dealt with at the same time.

As has been argued throughout *rEvolution*, a more holistic approach is often more helpful.

Intuitive thinking

Cue the more intuitive mindset or what many prefer to think of as "gut feel". Recently Gary Klein has done much to elevate intuition from the realms of supernatural soothsayers, prophets of doom, psychics and people who are determined to avoid the fruits of scientific discovery.

Klein describes intuition as "the way we translate our experiences into judgments and decisions. It's the ability to make decisions by using patterns to recognise what's going on in a situation and to recognise the typical action script with which to react. Once experienced intuitive decision makers see the pattern, any decision that they have to make is usually obvious."

Intuitive thinking enables us to take in many different sources of data at the same time. It is non-conscious. Klein coined the phrase "thin slicing" to describe this process. He tells the story of a Cleveland fire officer who managed to evacuate his team just before a building collapsed. Klein explains how he is processing, in a split second, a wide range of previously acquired knowledge of which he is not consciously aware. Malcolm Gladwell uses the word "blink" to encapsulate this same phenomenon in a single word.

You don't have to have been a firefighter to have had powerful moments of intuition; most of us have. Perhaps it was in a life or death situation like this (in which case its evolutionary benefits are clear). But more likely it will have been associated with some significant potential change in our life. Should we marry this person? Should we, sadly, divorce this person? Is this new house right for us? Should I accept this seemingly attractive job offer?

Intuitive thinking works well in situations where you do not have time to "think", in a situation, like a burning fire, when things are changing rapidly, where the issue you are facing has too many variables to analyse simultaneously and where the elements which seem important are somehow hard to put into words or are ambiguous. Intuitive thinking works best when used in conjunction with more analytical approaches.

A mixture of intuitive and analytical approaches are often what is required, as Thomas Carlyle suggested as long ago as the nineteenth century: "The healthy understanding, we should say, is not the logical, argumentative, but the intuitive, for the end of understanding is not to prove and find reasons, but to know and believe."

Pretended scepticism

Another useful habit of mind may at first seem a little strange – pretended scepticism. A pure sceptic is someone who believes that knowledge of any kind is unattainable. She or he is doubtful and questioning about any supposed "fact". In the UK the word has been devalued by its association with Euroscepticism, the label given to a wide range of people who want Britain to have no formal part in Europe but to remain an island. Under this banner shelter some intelligent patriots and some out and out fruitcakes.

But I want to use scepticism so that its meaning is closer to the original Greek word, σκέπτομαι, meaning "to look around, consider". For me, sceptics are people who look around, consider and question. They do this regularly, remaining cheerfully open-minded about issues even when others have come to their own conclusions. If the being sceptical becomes the default, or worse still, the only habit of mind you can adopt, then clearly you may become deeply, irksomely unattractive to be with! Bertrand Russell wrote a witty essay entitled "On the Value of Scepticism" which plays with the idea usefully. Russell suggests that it is undesirable to believe a proposition when there is no ground whatever for supposing it true! He qualifies this by arguing that his scepticism amounts to no more than when the experts are agreed, the opposite opinion cannot be held to be certain; that when they are not agreed, no opinion can be regarded as certain by a non-expert; and that when they all hold that no sufficient grounds for a positive opinion exist, the ordinary man would do well to suspend his judgement. Russell's ultimate goal is to rip away the prejudice and confusion that, in his view, dogged life at the time of his writing in the genuine hope that a happier world could be created.

Pretended scepticism is, however, different. It's an all-important evolutionary act of measured cunning, desired to help the whole human tribe avoid the bear-traps they are otherwise likely to fall into: "I really like the way you are … but I just wondered if …", "It's great you are thinking about doing … let me know if you want to think more about …". Pretended scepticism does not exclude optimism. It just helps to ensure that people do not run away with an idea by allowing it suddenly to be presented as truth without being able to challenge them.

The *Oxford English Dictionary* even has a word for this concept, to "scepticise", which it cites as being used in 1698 in the sense of "playing the sceptic". So, if you like this idea, get ready to scepticise!

Scenario creating

Along with the application of harder or softer thinking in deciding about any potential courses of action, we also need to be able to consider possible scenarios without committing to them. We need to play "What if?" and follow trains of thought through. Some people undoubtedly find this easier than others. So, for example, for one person, simply talking about doing something in the future seems like the beginnings of a commitment to act, while for another it is an intelligent way of applying the mind to what might be and is simply one of a number of options.

Successful adapters are good at the art of the possible, at the scenario-creating habit of mind. In a sense this is an aspect of living with ambiguity, similar to the kinds of issues we raised in Rule 4. In the 1990s, at Royal Dutch Shell, much use was made of a specific kind of scenario planning to help the company predict the future of petroleum and the actions of its competitors. Shell considered those things that it thought were predetermined events (the amount of crude oil in the ground) and those areas which were uncertainties (the impact of the Green movement).

There is no one way of doing scenario planning, but most processes involve some kind of detailed analysis, followed by a period of "What if?" idea generation. This leads to the production of half a dozen or more potential scenarios which, in turn, are broken down into two or three. This smaller number is then developed in much more detail.

As I write this we are in the midst of a global recession brought on, initially, by bad loans made by banks, mainly in the US, against houses owned by people who were always going to be unlikely to pay for them. Almost no one in the world is unaffected. "What if?" processes might be a helpful process to go through as an individual to determine your response to this external change. Will you decide to invest in government bonds, buy property because it is cheap, shift your pension into something safer than stocks and shares or spend your way out of recession? For each one of these you could construct some possible scenarios. And simply by going through this process you may be better able to ride out difficult times, clearer about which trends to resist and which seem, on balance, to make sense to you.

Patterns of social interaction

One way of ensuring that you are in tune with social movements and able to consider the merits or otherwise of new ideas is through debate and dialogue with as many other people as you can manage (while still saying sane!). In the last few years new websites and blogs have sprung up which make the process of exchanging ideas very straightforward.

Charles Leadbeater has recently written about the new world of mass innovation in *We-think*. (Actually the book's author is amusingly described as "Charles Leadbeater and 257 other people" which makes you realise one of his main points.) As we will explore in more detail in the next Rule, the web is changing the way we view knowledge and how it can be shared. It is challenging the idea that knowledge is power and replacing it with the notion of sharing knowledge as the most powerful kind of creativity.

There are people and organisations on the web which actively facilitate the exchange of information and new thinking, often hosted by whichever organisation is the lead body for the topic under discussion. These seem to be great places to have bookmarked as favourites and spend time in. Frequently debates on such sites seem like a gathering of sceptics anonymous, as they are excellent places to share niggles, doubts and concerns about views which seem to be gaining in credibility unreasonably! Allied to these are sites which provide weekly digests of interesting articles from across the globe on certain topics.

The Edge Foundation already mentioned in this Rule is a good example of a site interested in exploring big ideas in the US. By the same token, to take an example of an organisation with which I am associated, if you were interested in finding out more about how people adapt and develop then you might sign up to the UK's Talent Foundation (www.talentfoundation.com) and receive a weekly helping of half a dozen or so selected items. Sites like these are clever in other ways in that they use a kind of evolutionary software which constantly monitors what its users are enjoying. So, if they are reading articles on, say, evolution rather than on global finance, clever software on the site will search out more pieces on this theme so that users can explore issues in more detail.

Of course, some people prefer their social networking to be face to face, either by temperament or because so much of their working day is spent in front of a screen. The resurgence of the "coffee house" on the high street over the last decade has facilitated social networking by providing hospitable spaces and good coffee. And a number of organisations provide more organised opportunities for staying in touch with leading edge thinking.

In the UK, the RSA (Royal Society for the Encouragement of the Arts, Manufactures and Commerce), founded by William Shipley in the eighteenth century, has been preeminent in bringing together its global fellowship to interact with new ideas. In London and in a number of regions in the UK you can go to lectures and engage in debate, both analytical and intuitive, all broadly speaking designed to improve the lot of humankind. A kind of evolution of ideas, if you like. The RSA currently has 27,000 fellows and, along with a free public lecture programme, a range of innovative projects including reshaping the school curriculum, rethinking prison learning and developing new ways of approaching design, sustainable development, public services and the future of business!

Rule 7 – The argument so far

Not all change is helpful and successful adapters sometimes resist it. We need to be sure about our level of dissatisfaction with the status quo and certain that our prescription for improving it involves both a bigger vision and some practical first steps. Sometimes simply by challenging an idea we can help to shape and improve it. Habits of mind helpful to this process include analytical thinking, intuitive thinking, pretended scepticism and scenario creating. And in an increasingly networked world, to be actively part of its social networks for at least part of your time seems a sensible kind of interaction to encourage.

Last words:

> If people were to think together in a coherent way, it would have tremendous power.

> David Bohm

Rule 8 – Use the brainpower of those around you

We are in an era where the ideas of a single person alone seldom lead to fruition. All ideas originate with individuals, but their ideas must fit in with a matrix of innovation before progress is made.

Sir Alec Broers

Six degrees and a flat world

The foundation of democracy is faith in the capacities of human nature; faith in human intelligence and in the power of pooled and cooperative experience. It is not belief that these things are complete but that if given a show they will grow and be able to generate progressively the knowledge and wisdom needed to guide collective action.

John Dewey

As human beings have evolved there has always been a tension between tribe and individual. Groups seem to need leaders and tribes are often competitive. Thus many people end up believing that competition is the only way of proving their evolutionary credentials. So pernicious is this meme that collaboration is somehow seen as an admission that you as an individual do not have what it takes.

In schools, where many of society's attitudes are, of course, reflected, it is still very rare for pupils to be assessed as part of a group or for their specific teamworking skills. Indeed imitating others (often a smart thing to do) is seen as a kind cheating, and group work, while often used as a legitimate learning method, is viewed with suspicion by many. "How much of this group's successful work were you personally responsible for?" is the lurking question in the teacher's brain. The main occasion when children get assessed for their collaborative skills is through the medium of team sports where they win, lose or sometimes draw!

This old idea, that collaboration and imitation is a form of cheating, is deeply embedded and increasingly pernicious. Being able to adapt and thrive absolutely requires us to be able to get the best out of not just the resources afforded by the physical environment in which we find ourselves, but also the human resources with whom we are engaging.

Even as the earth's population continues to expand scarily beyond six billion people, and the planet becomes more and more populous, we are still deeply connected. The idea of "six degrees of separation" most potently captures our extraordinary interconnectedness and has entered the public imagination. Normally credited to John Guare's play, and the subsequent film of the same name, this proposes the idea that any two people can be connected by at most five other people. You know someone who knows someone who is married to someone who was friends with someone who went to the same school as X's mother. And in today's socially networked society it is even easier to find the small number of degrees that separate us from our fellow human beings.

The idea of the flat world has similarly entered our consciousness – in this case largely because of Thomas Friedman's book *The World is Flat* – to further confirm the connectedness of people. In this case it is the extraordinary phenomenon of global trade that is being highlighted. The world is flat in the sense that old barriers that would have made it difficult for me to trade with someone on the other side of the globe have vanished. I can, for example, design something in Sweden, for a company based in England, manufacture it in India and sell it in the US. I can do all of this because of Google and its ilk. Wherever I am in the world I can access the same information as anyone else. As a result of what Friedman lists as open-sourcing, offshoring, supply-chaining and many other ways in which it no longer matters where things are done or made, the world is, in one sense, flat.

The collective mind

Much earlier in *rEvolution* we looked at the way in which our brains are set up to make connections – how this is the way that we make sense of the data we take in. This is not just a neurobiological truth but a more profound one with regard to the way we organise information. As the poet Robert Frost once put it, "An idea is a feat of association, and the height of it is a good metaphor." From disparate ideas we create new concepts both linguistically and practically. A drop of blood becomes a "damned spot" in *Macbeth*. Steel, steam and the concept of travel lead us to invent the railway in the nineteenth century. And so on.

Indeed, metaphors and metaphorical ways of thinking shape our world view. My subheading, "the collective mind" implies, for example, a view of intelligence that suggests that it is shared across many people, and not solely resident in one person's head. In their seminal book, *Metaphors We Live by*, George Lakoff and Mark Johnson explore the way that metaphorical language shapes (and indicates) our world view. "Terrorist", "freedom fighter" and "murderer" are examples of words which could be used, with very different meanings depending on our standpoint, to describe brutal acts depending on our standpoint. The concept of evolution itself declares a world view which implies that adaptation is ubiquitous and that fixity is likely to be less successful as a strategy than flexibility.

How we connect with one thing or one idea with another matters. How we connect with other people is arguably even more important. This is not a new idea. In the 1920s Edward Thorndike first created the idea of "social intelligence". He identified three aspects of intelligence, abstract, mechanical and social. He defined social intelligence as being able to act wisely in human relations. More recently Howard Gardner's concept of interpersonal intelligence broadly follows this, distinguishing helpfully between intrapersonal (our ability to make sense of and manage our thoughts and feelings) and interpersonal (the capacity for people to do this collectively). And Gardner has gone on from here to talk of an ethical mind where the goal is to do "good works".

As the planet's population grows and the availability of resources shrinks, collaborative activity is becoming evolutionarily (and I would argue morally) ever more important if we are to survive as a species. Climate change and dwindling oil supplies, arguably the biggest challenge facing us all today, can only be solved through collective thought and cooperative action. Gardner has recently developed his own thinking to include different kinds of "mind", one of which is the "ethical mind". Thinking ethically requires us to go beyond our experience as an individual, but, as it were, to look at our actions from the perspective of the planet as a whole. It is not enough to consider whether a particular act is likely to help one person flourish; we need to consider the whole ecosystem at the same time. To behave ethically we have – individually, in groups and as a species – to reach a greater consensus on what constitutes "good works" and see the performance of these as the key to our survival.

In this context collaboration becomes a way of being. It is impossible to act individually without ethical consideration for the needs of others. Nature is of course full of examples of symbiosis or mutual cooperation: plant pollen, for instance, is transported by bees for which it is nourishment, and cleaner fish rid the mouths of sharks of rotting food. You scratch my back and I'll scratch yours!

In terms of human behaviour, social psychologists have developed the idea of the reciprocity principle, the idea that if we are offered a favour we want to repay it. This works at all levels of our lives. Think of the times, for example, when you have bought some new cheese after being offered a free sample of it as you wandered around a supermarket. Or accosted by someone in the street offering you a flower you find yourself reaching in your pocket for a coin to give her in return. Giving someone even a small something confers a kind of obligation on us to reciprocate.

A famous experiment illustrates this principle further. Two researchers sent Christmas cards to a group of people all of whom were complete strangers. Twenty per cent of people responded by sending Christmas cards back to the researchers, even though they did not know them! Why did they do this? Because the receipt of a gift, however small, triggers an instinctive response. We want to return the favour.

Although this kind of behaviour exists in the animal kingdom, it is, according to archaeologist Richard Leakey, at the heart of what it is to be human. In tribes the giving and sharing of food with strangers, for example, is a powerful example of social capital at work. Giving and receiving time, skills and resources confers indebtedness and binds us all together.

A powerful metaphor which enshrines these ideas is "coevolution". Stewart Brand, creator of the now defunct *CoEvolution Quarterly*, put it like this: "Evolution is adapting to meet one's needs. Coevolution, the larger view, is adapting to meet each other's needs."

Cooperation pays, as a famous game, Prisoner's Dilemma, shows. In this game the following scenario is imagined. Two people are arrested on suspicion of having committed a crime. The police have insufficient evidence for a conviction, so they separate the prisoners. They then approach each one separately to offer the same deal. If one testifies for the prosecution against the other, and the other remains silent, the betrayer will go free while the silent accomplice will receive a full ten-year sentence. If both keep quiet, both prisoners will be sentenced to only six months in jail for a minor charge. If they both betray each other, each will receive a five-year sentence. Each person has to choose whether to betray the other or to remain silent. Each one is told that the other will not know about any betrayal. The question is: how should the prisoners act?

The answer? It depends! Those who have explored this and other similar games (like Robert Axelrod in *The Evolution of Cooperation*) suggest that if the game is played just once then the incentive for one person to grass on the other may be too tempting. However, if the game is played many times then the smart evolutionary strategy is to find the closest thing to a win-win strategy and for both prisoners to keep quiet and accept the short six-month sentence.

A simple game I like that demonstrates the wisdom of planned cooperation is this. Imagine you have a group of people. Ask them to stand in pairs facing each other and raise their right arm. Get them to grasp the other person's hand and knot their fingers together. The game is to see how many times one of the players can force the other person's hand back against his or her shoulder. The winner will be the person who does this more times than any other in the room in the space of thirty seconds.

Most people immediately see this as a competitive challenge and much pushing and pulling takes place with a hand occasionally being forced back onto a shoulder. Scores are low. Gradually participants realise that all they need to do is to cooperate and stop flexing their muscles. After a few seconds these couples are smoothly taking it in turns, with no muscular resistance, to "force" their partner's hand willingly onto their shoulder!

In a complex world, cooperation is ever more important. Dealing with change rarely relies on one individual alone. Earlier, when we touched on the idea of the learning organisation, we saw how this necessarily involves systems thinking. Management expert Warren Bennis goes further: "The major challenge for leaders in the 21st century will be to release the brainpower of their organisations." One brain is not enough; we need to harness our collective capability to adapt and thrive. Successful organisations today need distributed brainpower and what is increasingly being referred to as "distributed leadership". In the UK the National College of School Leadership has been promoting the idea that leadership from the middle can contribute to significant improvements in the learning experiences of pupils. By the same token, influenced by the work of Jean Lave and Etienne Wenger (see Rule 5), health services across the world have begun to see the value of engaging those closest to patients, often the nurse on the ward, in helping to design better ways of improving the quality of patient care. And to ensure that local ideas are informed by the best in the world, individuals can be part of communities of practice which can literally or virtually bring together people doing similar things to share ideas.

If you agree that our only real hope in solving the problems of a complex and changing organism like the world we live in is through collaboration, then the inescapable conclusions you will come to is that we need to get better at working together in groups. (See later in this Rule where I explore the idea of facilitation.) We need a new belief in the value of public learning and of the power of thoughtful groups. This is not the same thing as the wisdom or folly of the crowd (see Rule 7). Crowds which don't talk properly to each other can too often get things wrong, for through the use of well-judged processes it is possible to minimise any negative aspects of groupthinking.

At the level of the family we also need to find ways of breaking cycles of poor evolution. As I write, the UK is considering how it will raise the school leaving age to 18 (it is currently possible to leave at 16 although many stay on until 17). Skilfully the UK government has reframed the challenge as "raising the participation age", realising that participating in learning is a much more positive concept than the implied compulsion and childishness of the "school leaving age". For many young people are happy to learn but not necessarily at school.

Indeed this is what I, with my co-director Guy Claxton, are intent in thinking through at the new Centre for Real-World Learning at the University of Winchester. How can we get better at helping people to get better at learning the things that matter in their lives? How have we managed to allow such a large fault line to appear between academic and practical learning? How can we nurture generations who love making as much as they like thinking and who see acting and reflecting as complementary activities? If young people have fallen out of love with learning in their early teens, how can they thrive in the kind of world that I am describing?

Gregory Bateson went straight to the heart of this issue when he identified a dilemma which we often experience: "In the transmission of human culture, people always attempt to replicate, to pass on to the next generation the skills and values of the parents, but the attempt always fails because cultural transmission is geared to learning, not DNA."

In the tribes of the savannah, learning and doing, surviving a hunt and gathering edible berries must have been complementary aspects of telling fireside stories of derring-do and mentoring or initiating younger members of the group into the ways of survival. Shared learning was indistinguishable from shared living.

And it is learning which sits at the heart of successful evolution and adaption to change for us all today. In particular it is our capacity to combine our own ability to learn better with an enhanced disposition to share this capacity with many others, so creating knowledge and wisdom.

Habits of mind

Certain dispositions will serve us better as we endeavour to use the brainpower of those around us.

Pitching in

Barbara Rogoff has a simple concept to describe the natural way in which younger members of families and groups learn by trying things out. She calls it "pitching in". In the communities she has observed, often the uneconomically developed ones of Africa and South America, she observes the ways in which very young children watch their parents and elder siblings doing household chores, planting seeds, gathering and cooking food and then just pitch in themselves confident that they can learn how to do these things in a secure environment. The consequence of the shared learning in communities like this is that children have learned all the skills they need for survival by as early as seven years old. Contrast this with the developed world where even teenagers would struggle to grow or cook food!

Rogoff has demonstrated the value of learning through keen observation and listening, in anticipation of participation. She calls this kind of learning "intent participation". It is how, for example, much first language learning takes place. She contrasts this with what she calls "assembly line instruction" where knowledge is transmitted by an adult teacher. It is a kind of informal apprenticeship which has been surprisingly little researched but which is a method we use throughout our lives.

Evolutionarily speaking, Rogoff takes us back to valuable aspects of the learning journey that the human species has travelled. As Robert Hutchins reminds us: "Education was not a segregated activity, conducted for certain hours, in certain places, at a certain time of life. It was the aim of society." Nowadays in the developed world we separate children from the adult world when we send them to school and, perhaps most significantly, we separate them from much of our working lives. The exception to this situation is when one or more parents works from home or if there is some kind of family business, like a restaurant, shop, farm or garage. In these cases, although health and safety inspectors make it more difficult, children see at first hand how their parents do their work tasks. Rogoff describes a telling interview with a 12-year-old girl who has already learned how to use a sharp knife because she has spent hours watching her father and then pitched in with increasingly sharp knives.

Systematically losing the daily interaction between adult work and children seems to have removed a valuable element of family learning. I am not suggesting for a moment that we should return to any kind of child exploitation, but the artificial separation we have contrived in the developed world, especially in the US and Europe, seems to deny young people hours of valuable informal tutelage. Having young minds set to "pitch in" and try things out with their family and in their local community seems to be exactly the kind of habit to encourage, rather than artificially dividing up the worlds of family and school, home and work.

Sociability (sometimes)

It's axiomatic of any sense of collective action that people need to be sociable enough with each other to the extent that it is likely that they will share thoughts and opinions! In some neighbourhoods you can all too easily spot the fast walk and determined avoidance of eye contact to know that it is not the kind of place where people stop and chat. In others you have only to pause for a moment and look slightly lost and several friendly people will come up and offer assistance.

If we wish to be likely to learn from those around us, then being sociable is undoubtedly a useful habit of mind for all of us to develop – with two caveats. The first is, as we saw in Rules 2 and 3, that we also need time for ourselves to build our own inner well of creativity, and the second simply involves a recognition that more introverted people may find sociability harder to cultivate. Interestingly, the advent of blogging has given many people who might previously have described themselves as shy or introverted a chance to contribute their ideas without embarrassment – a kind of online sociability.

Human beings have always needed to and wanted to live in groups. This is fine for the group itself but the danger is that, when all groups are threatened, for example by the lack of a resource like water, then the group mentality becomes more territorial and tribal. Add in religion to the mix and we are in dangerous times. Finding sociability within this context is today's challenge.

We may need to go backwards to what was first meant by *commonwealth*, for the original meaning "common-wealth" or "the common weal" in the fifteenth century had to do with the old meaning of "wealth" – "well-being". So common-wealth suggested "common well-being". A commonwealth was, therefore, a state governed for the common good as opposed to one led for the benefit of a few members.

Sociability as an attitude of mind requires us not just to use each other's brainpower, but also to acknowledge and take care of each other. Later in this Rule we will touch on a practical example of how these kinds of principles are being put into practice in local communities. Indeed, given the difficulty of changing the opinions of some of the global tribes as it were by megaphone, berating one group for not believing what we think, it may well be that rebuilding common well-being at a local level is where we need to start.

Another word that may need some rehabilitation, along with commonwealth, is neighbourliness. A recent pamphlet from the Smith Institute explores the decline in neighbourliness which it helpfully describes as "the exchange of small services or support in an emergency against a background of routine convivial exchanges". There is, in other words, a component of socialising – convivial exchanges which start in the street and end up over the kitchen table – and reciprocal help and support. In truth neighbourliness is as much an orientation or habit of mind as it is a behaviour. It involves the cultivation of a set of beliefs about the value of mutually interdependent living.

Empathy

For any community to work we need to know what its members are thinking. In a local democracy we can find this out occasionally through the ballot box. But this is not enough. On a daily basis it involves empathy.

Empathy is the ability to walk in another person's shoes and see the world as they see it. It involves the capacity to experience things vicariously. To do this we need to be able not only to hear what people say but read their non-verbal communication. In a violent world such as the one we live in an excess of empathy can lead one to nervous depression or a lack of it to callousness. In our everyday lives it is going to be somewhere in between.

As a habit of mind it requires us routinely to wonder what things look like from another perspective. Throughout *rEvolution* we have seen how direct experience is a powerful tool for changing minds. So too is vicarious experience. In Rule 6 we even saw how extreme phobias could be dealt with vicariously. In recent years television soap operas have shown the power of dramatic vicarious experience by exploring issues such as sexuality, AIDS and illiteracy through their storylines, only to find themselves creating a surge of interest in a previously misunderstood issue.

In Rule 5 we briefly mentioned mirror neurons, cells which suggest that human beings may be prewired to empathise with others. First discovered by Giaccamo Rizzolatti in the frontal lobes of monkeys, mirror neurons are activated both when a monkey does something itself and when it watches another monkey doing the same thing. Researchers using neuro-imaging techniques have recently found similar effects in human beings. The existence of such "empathy neurons", seemingly explicitly designed to support imitative activity, has led to profound debates about when and how, evolutionarily speaking, such a shift occurred in the human brain. But the fact remains that there is a neurological as well as psychological argument for the value of empathy.

One of the simplest and at the same time most profound ways in which we signal the degree of empathetic engagement is through the language we use. There's nothing new about this line of thought, as Ecclesiastes 27:5–7 describes:

"Its fruit discloses the cultivation of a tree; so a person's speech discloses the cultivation of his mind." This kind of thinking is summed up in the Sapir–Whorf Hypothesis, which suggests that the nature and structure of any particular language governs the patterns of speech used by its speakers. Some linguists would go further and subscribe to a kind of linguistic determinism that suggests that what we are able to put into words is constrained by the structure of the language we are using. Great writers who bust the conventions of their language are proof of the limitation of this kind of view, but nevertheless, at a personal level, our default verbal responses strongly indicate the degree to which we are prone to empathy or single vantage point living:

"You're wrong …"

"It can't be like that …"

"The answer to this is …"

Contrast these with more empathetic responses such as:

"I wonder if he …"

"She might be thinking that …"

"I really understand where you are coming from but wondered if …"

If we want to release the brain power of those around us, the more we can use responsible and respectful language, the more likely we are to achieve this.

Tool – Empathise!

Explore your own emotions:
Being aware of your own feelings is the essential first step.

Look and read:
Put yourself in the other person's shoes. How are they feeling? Check that you have read their emotional state.

Listen:
Listen carefully. Check that what is being said matches with what you are picking up from body language.

Imagine:
Use any clues to put yourself in their shoes and feel what they are feeling.

Some people seem naturally to be able to empathise; for others it takes conscious practice. But it is definitely a learnable habit of mind.

Collaboration

Recently the Massachusetts Institute of Technology launched the Center for Collective Intelligence (www.cci.mit.edu) to explore this big question: how can people and computers be connected so that – collectively – they act more intelligently than any individuals, groups or computers have ever done before?

It's a good question and MIT has chosen predominantly to explore the online aspects of this by looking at the phenomenon of searching, especially Google, and wikinomics, the ability for large groups to input their thoughts into a single emerging document. The centre is trying to create new examples of collective intelligence – for example, the Climate Collaboratorium (a project seeking to harness the brainpower of thousands of people to solve the issue of global climate change) – while at the same time developing theories of collective intelligence in its *Handbook of Collective Intelligence.* While the Internet undoubtedly opens up new opportunities for people to work together in ways that were never possible before, I am as much interested in the patterns of face-to-face social interaction which might facilitate this.

The thrust of these initiatives is on "we" not "I" – the "we-think" of Charles Leadbeater mentioned in Rule 7. We need structures and approaches that flow from the strongly held belief that, to adapt and thrive, collaboration is a necessity not an option! Individuals have a huge amount to contribute but the power of collaborative action is so much greater. As Paul Hawken and colleagues put it in *Seven Tomorrows*, a report of the Stanford Futures Research Group: "We need a collective intelligence of a kind that may have not characterized the human species in the past."

Collective intelligence calls upon high-level collaboration skills and a mindset that sees collaboration as essential. Core to this is good teamworking and, in particular, the cultivation of certain processes, especially a broad repertoire of conflict resolution methods which are effective in groups whatever the specific dynamic of that group.

In a period of change and instability, such as the one we are living through, a key attribute in terms of collaboration is the ability to manage a large number of short-term relationships. Business and social networking organisations abound to help us here, but I am thinking more of the personal confidence and resourcefulness required to establish and maintain a significant number of short-term but valuable relationships.

Patterns of social interaction

In the old world much social interaction was highly structured and often largely about control. Teachers stood at the front of classes and instructed children. Children were seen but ideally not heard. Leaders issued commands from on high. Businesses and civil services were run through hierarchical and highly formalised knowledge transmission routes from top to bottom.

As the great American educator Jerome Bruner put it in *The Culture of Education*: "What we have learned in recent years about human learning [is] that it is at its best when it is participatory, proactive, communal, collaborative, and given over to constructing meanings rather than receiving them."

All is changing today. Where once we relied on teaching and telling, today we need facilitation and learning. And it is by focusing on different styles of facilitation that I want to end *rEvolution*. A facilitator is someone skilled in learning methods and group dynamics, who makes it easier for groups of people to work and learn together for an agreed purpose. I don't think I had even heard of the word "facilitation" until a decade or so ago. Yet now, as a professional facilitator, I am routinely engaged to facilitate groups of people by private, public and third sector organisations. Why does anyone want to hire a facilitator? In essence, to help them extract the maximum collective brainpower from their people, to engage them in constructing rather than receiving meaning.

Facilitation has emerged from a number of parallel developments in business, education, counselling, religious and community development. In some ways one can trace the beginnings of facilitative approaches in Britain back to the eighteenth century and philosopher John Locke's assertion that everyone had the right to participate in decisions that affect their life and community. For about the same period of time the Religious Society of Friends (the Quakers) have used a combination of prayerful silence and facilitation, often by an elder, to achieve consensus about complex issues. In the US, much useful thinking was undertaken in the area of community development by Sherry Arnstein who brought to the concept of facilitation the parallel idea of participation and explored its meaning in terms of real engagement at a grassroots level.

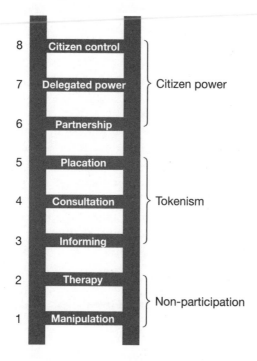

In education there is about a century of active interest in facilitation with John Dewey arguing, as above, in a very

modern sounding way, that teachers should be more facilitative. Maria Montessori also espoused such approaches. In
the 1970s Carl Rogers took education into new realms with
his use of facilitators to help individuals remove the barriers to learning, building on his earlier work on client-centred counselling. At the radical end of thinking Ivan Illich
famously suggested that we should de-school society and
find new ways of facilitating learning at a community level
and Paulo Freire introduced a method of consciousness-rais-
ing among oppressed people, using facilitators, that would
help them remove the fear they might otherwise have felt in
formal educational settings controlled by the state.

In the business world the interest in facilitation arguably
began with the advent of mass production and large groups
of people involved in workplaces. As managerial systems
have evolved there has always been a tension between managers chairing meetings (and potentially getting their own
way) and groups of workers being facilitated to come up
with the best answer, so harnessing their collective intelligence. In the last five decades an interest in the generation
of ideas (e.g. Alex Osborn coined the term "brainstorming"
some fifty years ago) and in the process of quality improvement has necessitated a greater focus on the process by
which ideas are turned into action.

A parallel enrichment of the idea of facilitation has been
brought about by David Bohm and his thinking about dialogue as a means of finding solutions to the challenges we
face in our lives:

> It is proposed that a form of free dialogue may well
> be one of the most effective ways of investigating the
> crisis which faces society, and indeed the whole of
> human nature and consciousness today. Moreover,
> it may turn out that such a form of free exchange of
> ideas and information is of fundamental relevance

for transforming culture and freeing it of destructive misinformation, so that creativity can be liberated.

Bohn argued passionately for ways of creating meaning that allow different points of view simply to "be" rather than trying to argue them out.

Two approaches to facilitation

Today we have a deep well of ideas for facilitation from which we can drink. Here are just a few examples. Through facilitation conflicts can be ended, a sense of purpose can be created collaboratively, complex issues can be understood better and people's creativity can be unleashed. In Rule 4, I introduced the idea of appreciative inquiry and to conclude *rEvolution* I want to mention two other important processes.

World Café

World Café (www.theworldcafe.com) is the development of an idea that is as old as the hills – that we talk and think at our best when we are sitting round a table sharing food and drink. Its approach to knowledge sharing assumes that conversations flows better in a friendly café setting than in formal meetings in airless rooms. There is no set methodology, although a typical assumption would be that conversations would be held between people sitting at small tables.

Typically a room is set up to resemble a café with round tables with table cloths, flowers and water (or something stronger!). Once the context is clear, with everyone understanding why they are there and what the purpose of the session is, the process involves a series of table conversations with every effort being made to connect the diverse viewpoints of participants. A particularly useful aspect of the process is the convention that one or two members of each table move to another table at the "end" of each conversation. The next conversation then starts by asking those who have just joined a table to share their conversational insights and vice versa. Each table is lightly hosted to ensure that no one person dominates the talking. Through World Café real listening is encouraged so that new patterns and new knowledge is created and shared.

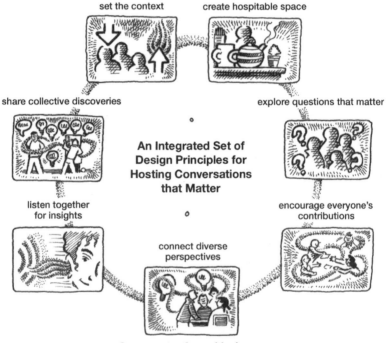

set the context

create hospitable space

share collective discoveries

An Integrated Set of Design Principles for Hosting Conversations that Matter

explore questions that matter

listen together for insights

encourage everyone's contributions

connect diverse perspectives

Source: www.theworldcafe.com

As political journalist William Greider helpfully says: "Creating a positive future begins in human conversation. The simplest and most powerful investment any member of a community or an organisation may make in renewal is to begin talking with other people as though the answers mattered."

Open Space

Open Space (www.openspaceworld.org), sometimes called Open Space Technology, is another powerful means of bringing groups of people together, especially large ones. Initially created by Harrison Owen, Open Space is the antidote to a conventional conference or meeting where expert input is delivered to delegates and participants have only occasional moments, often only in structured question and answer formats, to make their input. In Open Space the participants *are* the event, hosting and taking part in a large number of parallel sessions exploring a collaboratively agreed question or theme.

Open Space needs a large room where it is possible to have all participants sitting in a large circle (or concentric circles if this is easier). Open space facilitators run sessions using four principles and one law. The four principles are:

1. Whoever comes is the right person.

2. Whatever happens is the only thing that could have.

3. Whenever it starts is the right time.

4. When it is over it is over.

Like the principles the law is a slightly folksy saying called "the law of two feet". More than anything this defines the spirit of open space. Essentially this means that participants need to go to where they feel they can make a difference. Conversely, everyone should feel free to go to whichever meeting they wish to and not feel compelled to stay in a conversation or session which is not working for them. You get out what you put in. You are a voluntary member of any group and just as responsible as everyone else for making it work well.

While at first the law and the principles may seem like a recipe for selfish anarchy, in practice it works in reverse – for anyone hosting a session is at pains to check that he or she is engaging those taking part. It also breeds a creative cross-pollination of thinking as some people buzz from one group and another.

Most open space sessions start informally as people gather and then, when everyone is ready, sit in a large circle. People introduce themselves, sometimes with a short story about themselves, either to the whole group or to smaller sections of that group. Once the theme is introduced by the facilitator, then all that is required is a simple mechanism for people to be able to host sessions throughout the time allocated for these.

Session title	
Host	
Location	
Time	
Members	1 2 3 4 5 6

Facilitators will normally agree with participants on the overall number of sessions, but within this there can be flexibility for longer or shorter sessions. Hosts can indicate the number of participants they would like and the whole process can be managed either using a paper-based system or electronically.

Each session ideally produce something – a short report, a cartoon, a picture, a film clip, which they post around the room for others to enjoy. Sessions are rarely rounded off with any kind of formal plenary speeches but more often use some kind of community marketplace activity to enable people to circulate and share.

These two examples of contemporary approaches to facilitation are just the tip of the iceberg. Think also: participative service design (where the users of services help their creators to improve their design and delivery); deliberative workshops (where local people are given the same access to high quality information as local politicians get and meet to listen and think their way through complex issues); and experiential deep ecology (as practised, for example, by Joanna Macy (www.joannamacy.net) with its strong Buddhist traditions and overtly emotional engagement with issues). At a local level the work of the Transition Towns movement (www.transitiontowns.org), created by Rob Hopkins in the UK, is the closest thing I have found that seeks to create the kind of dynamic, coevolutionary patterns of social interaction at a community level which are designed to promote the harvesting of collective brainpower along with good stewardship of the planet. And a virtual example of this kind of thinking can be found at the Co-Intelligence Institute (www.co-intelligence.org).

Rule 8 – The argument so far

The survival of the planet depends on human beings working together to release their collective brainpower. As our numbers grow towards seven billion, and as traditional resources such as oil diminish, this will become more not less urgent. Habits of mind helpful to this process include pitching in, sociability, empathy and collaboration. Socially, and most importantly, if we are to create a different kind of world in which our common survival is assured, then we all need to become confident and skilled in a range of facilitative methods. This is the collective mindware that we all need. A key outcome of formal schooling needs to be the cultivation of facilitative dispositions in every young person so that, as a society, we will be equipped to adapt to any new issue that we face.

Last words:

> Throughout history, the really fundamental changes in society have come about not from dictates of governments and the results of battles but through vast numbers of people changing their minds, sometimes only a little bit.
>
> Willis Harman

Rule 9 – Make up your own rules

Rules are not necessarily sacred, principles are.

Franklin D. Roosevelt

Any fool can make a rule and any fool will mind it.

Henry Thoreau

End piece

It's in the nature of people as they grow older to protest against change, particularly change for the better.

John Steinbeck

Thanks for making it through to the end of *rEvolution*!

Although maybe you didn't. Perhaps you started at the beginning and jumped to the last Rule or dipped into the middle and idly flicked your way through!

That's the irritating and wonderful thing about Homo sapiens. You can take us to the water but you can't make us drink. We are all different and we all view past, present and possible futures through personal lenses. And the sapiens/ thinking bit, as the quotation from John Steinbeck illustrates, is not strong enough always to propel us in the direction which is most sensible.

It's not powerful enough for the very important reason that we are creatures of habit. Changing our habits of mind is complex and hard, as anyone who has tried to make significant alterations to their lifestyle knows. We may know logically that too much air or car travel is not good for a planet under threat, but we are still likely to find it difficult to travel less, walk more or take the train. Or at a personal level, we may know that an excess of computer gadgetry can seriously damage our personal relationships, yet still interrupt important events like family mealtimes by allowing verbal or textual communications to be listened to or checked.

Let me return for a moment to Gleicher's formula which we met in Rule 7:

$$D \times V \times F > R$$

D = Dissatisfaction with how things are
V = Vision of what is possible
F = First, concrete steps that can be taken towards the vision
R = Resistance

The three letters – D, V and F – explain clearly why change is so hard. For while we may feel dissatisfaction, we may not have either vision or practical first steps. Or, perhaps more often, we have either vision or practical suggestions but not both.

From where I sit there is only one thing of which I am certain and that is that the world will continue to change. Within this statement of the obvious I guess there are three areas of near certainty:

1. The climate will continue to heat up (unless something remarkable happens).

2. The world's population will keep growing.

3. Computers will keep on getting smarter and providing us with wonderful supplementary mindware and some people will think that they are more important than the human mind.

It is not difficult to be dissatisfied with aspects of each of these three trends. But for each of them combining V and F remains challenging and complex. Not surprisingly, for some people this is all they need to confirm them in their resistance to change.

In helping you survive and hopefully thrive, I hope you feel that the eight "rules" – well nine if you count the lighthearted one in this end piece – *rEvolution*, along with their accompanying habits of mind and "patterns of social interaction" offer you some food for thought. But, of course, as the quotations at the start of this Rule suggest, you will want to make up your own set, or at the very least custom- ise mine. Depending on your own situation, some elements may connect with your experiences more than others.

The social dimension

If we are all going to be able to thrive harmoniously on the planet then we will need to be not Homo technians but Homo *per*sapiens (i.e. very wise men and women) and, per- haps most importantly, Homo socialis (i.e. cooperative, col- laborative and social).

Consequently the ideas which appear in the previous Rules are in many ways the most important ones. Indeed, the strong sense in which we are all interdependent underpins the inclusion of the patterns of social interaction throughout the book and which I have listed below so that you can see them as a whole:

- *Socialising with intent* – seeing the evolutionary value in watching and learning from others.

- *Knowing when to be social and when solitary* – remember- ing to look after and nurture your inner resources as well as looking outwards.

- *Social intuition* – getting better at "reading" social situ- ations, heeding your gut feel and acknowledging that your inklings and hunches may well have a validity.

- *Appreciative Inquiry* – bringing a questioning mind to all that you do, but staying positive and always look- ing for what is already going well rather than sinking into adversarial critique, and being prepared to dream on and remain idealistic.

- *Communities of practice* – ensuring that you are a member of expert groups, some of which interlock, some of which are discrete, and that learning to watch from the edge is a valuable evolutionary attribute as you practise.

- *Action learning* – combining enquiry with practicality and surrounding yourself with small groups of friends and colleagues who are prepared to help you work through issues and problems to find solutions, just as you, in turn, are ready to reciprocate.

- *Debate and dialogue* – as has always been the case, staying open to new ideas and being prepared to be rigorously analytical, all in the context of the socially networked world in which we live.

- *Facilitation* – actively using facilitative processes in all that you do so that you become more skilled at liberating the brainpower of those around you for the common good.

Each of these eight areas of interest carries with it much knowledge and research which I have not had time to explore; all I hope I might have done is to kindle or rekindle your wish to go and find out more.

Throughout *rEvolution* I have deliberately allowed Darwin's wonderful ideas about biological evolution over long periods of time to mingle with the idea that a contemporary Darwin might have had to revise his (or her) thinking about both the timescale of evolution and the degree to which people can be said to be able to influence the course of their evolution. If our mind is the central tool of our continued evolution, the organ at the heart of adaptive intelligence, then we need to look at our mindware with the perspective of the survival of our species.

Our minds are programmed to evolve during their lifetimes and such adaptation confers advantages to its owner while they are alive. But the real adaptive intelligence we need is socially constructed. It exists between people who, precisely because they have brains, can figure out collaborative ways of being and thriving.

Finding our tap roots

Remember the *Finding your tap root* tool on page 36? As individuals living in a complex and constantly evolving system (our planet) we have to find our own niche, to connect to the roots of what matters to us. We need, as Ken Robinson has suggested in *The Element: How Finding Your Passion Changes Everything*, to find the place where the things we love doing and the things we are good at combine. And, I would add, a place where we can be reasonably confident that what we are doing is ideally a force for good (or at least not for ill) insofar as we are able to see it.

For many years now I have been involved with the UK's Talent Foundation (www.talentfoundation.com) precisely because I care about the development of human potential. Our fundamental tenet is and continues to be that there is an abundance of talent on the earth and that it is our job as responsible members of the species to develop it both individually *and* collectively for the wider "tribe".

A century and a half ago, when Darwin's ideas were first being released into the wild, they were revolutionary. People either took to them as if they were a religion or took against them because they could not accommodate them into their own religion. Darwin was describing many millions of years of slow, random evolution. Today we do not have Darwin's guiding presence to make sense of what is happening. But we do have his spirit as we apply all the mindware available to us with his guiding principle of responsiveness.

I'd like to think, I hope not too fancifully, that while today's evolution may seem revolutionary to us if we are caught up in its white waters, what is happening in front of our eyes is really a revolution with a small "r". And we can use our adaptive intelligence to ensure that we survive and thrive in ways that are true to what we want to be as a species.

Last words:

> I was a young man with uninformed ideas. I threw out queries, suggestions, wondering all the time over everything; and to my astonishment the ideas took off like wildfire. People made a religion of them.
>
> Charles Darwin

Selected Bibliography

If you have liked any of the ideas in *rEvolution* you may enjoy going into more depth with some of these books, all of which I have found useful and interesting.

Argyris, Chris (1994). *Knowledge for Action* (San Francisco, CA: Jossey-Bass).

Arnstein, Sherry (1969). "A Ladder of Citizen Participation", *Journal of the American Institute of Planners* 35(4): 216–224.

Axelrod, Robert (1984). *The Evolution of Cooperation* (New York: Basic Books).

Bandura, Albert (1995). *Self-Efficacy in Changing Societies* (Cambridge: Cambridge University Press).

Bateson, Gregory (1972). *Steps to an Ecology of Mind: Collected Essays in Anthropology, Psychiatry, Evolution, and Epistemology* (Chicago: University of Chicago Press).

Bennis, Warren (2000). *Old Dogs, New Tricks* (London: Kogan Page).

Blackmore, Susan (1999). *The Meme Machine* (Oxford: Oxford University Press).

Bransford, John et al. (ed.) (2000). *How People Learn; Brain, Mind, Experience and School* (Washington: National Academy Press)

Bridges, William (2003). *Managing Transitions: Making the Most of Change* (Cambridge, MA: Da Capo Press).

Bronson, Po and Merryman, Ashley (2007). "How Not to Talk to Your Kids", *New York Magazine*, 19 Feb. 2007.

Bruner, Jerome (1996). *The Culture of Education* (Cambridge, MA: Harvard University Press).

Clark, Andy (2003). *Natural-Born Cyborgs; Minds, Technologies, and the Future of Human Intelligence* (Oxford: Oxford University Press).

Claxton, Guy (1997). *Hare Brain, Tortoise Mind: Why Intelligence Increases When You Think Less* (London: Fourth Estate).

Claxton, Guy and Lucas, Bill (2007). *The Creative Thinking Plan: How to Generate Ideas and Solve Problems in Your Work and Life* (London: BBC Active).

Cooperrider, David L. and Whitney, Diana (2005). *Appreciative Inquiry: A Positive Revolution in Change* (San Fransico: Berrett-Koehler)

Costa, Art and Kallick, Bena (2000). *Habits of Mind: A Developmental Series* (Alexandria, VA: Association for Supervision and Curriculum Development).

Covey, Stephen (1997). *The Seven Habits of Highly Effective Families* (London: Simon and Schuster).

Csikszentmihalyi, Mihalyi (1991). *Flow: The Psychology of Optimal Experience* (New York: HarperCollins).

Darwin, Charles (1859). *On the Origin of Species* (London: John Murray).

Dawkins, Richard (1967). *The Selfish Gene* (New York: Oxford University Press).

de Bono, Edward (1967). *The Use of Lateral Thinking* (London: Penguin).

Deming, W. Edwards (1986). *Out of the Crisis.* (Boston, MA: MIT Press).

Dennett, Daniel C. (1996). *Darwin's Dangerous Idea; Evolution and the Meanings of Life* (London: Penguin Books).

Dewey, John (1938). *Logic: The Theory of Inquiry* (New York: Holt and Company).

Dweck, Carol (2006). *Mindset; The New Psychology of Success* (New York: Ballantine Books).

English Project, The (2008). *Kitchen Table Lingo* (London: Virgin Books).

Ericsson, Anders (ed.) (2006). *The Road to Excellence; The Acquisition of Expert Performance in the Arts and Sciences, Sports, and Games* (Mahwah: Lawrence Erlbaum Associates).

Festinger, Leon, Riecken, Henry W. and Schachter, Stanley (1956). *When Prophecy Fails: A Social and Psychological Study of a Modern Group that Predicted the End of the World* (Minneapolis: University of Minnesota Press).

Friedman, Thomas (2005). *The World is Flat: The Globalized World in the Twenty-First* Century (New York: Farrar, Straus, and Giroux).

Gardner, Howard (2004). *Changing Minds: The Art and Science of Changing Our Own and Other People's Minds* (Cambridge, MA: Harvard Business School).

Gardner, Howard (2007). *Five Minds for the Future* (Cambridge, MA: Harvard Business School).

Gladwell, Malcolm (2000). *The Tipping Point: How Little Things Can Make a Big Difference* (London: Little, Brown and Company).

Gladwell, Malcolm (2005). *Blink: The Power of Thinking without Thinking* (London: Allen Lane).

Hallowell, Edward M. and Ratey, John J. (1995). *Driven to Distraction: Recognizing and Coping with Attention Deficit Disorder from Childhood through Adulthood* (New York: Touchstone).

Handy, Charles (1999). *The New Alchemists* (London: Hutchinson).

Harman, Willis (1998). *Global Mind Change; The Promise of the 21st Century* (San Francisco: Berrett-Koehler Publishers Inc).

Harvey, Jerry B. (1974). "The Abilene Paradox and Other Meditations on Management", *Organizational Dynamics* 3(1): 63–80.

Hawken, Paul, Ogilvy, James and Schwartz, Peter (1982). *Seven Tomorrows: Seven Scenarios for the Eighties and Nineties* (New York: Bantam).

Hill, Napoleon (1994). *Napoleon Hill's Keys to Success: The 17 Principles of Personal Achievement* (New York: Penguin).

Holt, John (1969). *How Children Fail* (London: Penguin Books).

Hoffer, Eric (1963). *The Ordeal of Change* (New York: Harper & Row).

Holmes, T. H. and Rahe, R. H. (1967). "The Social Readjustment Rating Scale", *Journal of Psychosomatic Research* 11(2): 213–221.

Honey, Peter and Mumford, Alan (1992). *The Manual of Learning Styles* (Maidenhead: Peter Honey Publications).

Honoré, Carl (2004). *In Praise of Slow: How a Worldwide Movement Is Challenging the Cult of Speed* (London: Orion).

Hutchins, Robert M. (1953). *The University of Utopia* (Chicago: University of Chicago Press).

James, William (1890). *The Principles of Psychology* (Boston, MA: Harvard University Press).

Klein, Gary (1999). *Sources of Power: How People Make Decisions* (Cambridge, MA: MIT Press).

Kuhn, Thomas (1962). *The Structure of Scientific Revolutions* (Chicago: University of Chicago Press).

Lakoff, George and Johnson, Mark (1980). *Metaphors We Live By* (Chicago: University of Chicago Press).

Langer, Ellen (1997). *The Power of Mindful Learning* (Reading, MA: Perseus Books).

Lave, Jean and Wenger, Etienne (1991). *Situated learning; legitimate peripheral participation* (Cambridge: Cambridge University Press).

Leadbeater, Charles (2000). *Living On Thin Air: The New Economy* (Harmondsworth: Penguin).

Leadbeater, Charles (2008). *We-think* (London: Profile Books).

Lewin, Kurt (1997). *Resolving Social Conflicts; Field Theory in Social Science* (Washington: American Psychological Association).

Locke, Edwin and Latham, Gary (1990). *A Theory of Goal Setting and Task Performance* (Englewood Cliffs, NJ: Prentice Hall).

Lucas, Bill (2006). *Boost Your Mind Power Week by Week* (London: Duncan Baird).

Lucas, Bill (2001). *Power Up Your Mind: Learn Faster, Work Smarter* (London: Nicholas Brealey).

Martin, James (2006). *The Meaning of the 21st Century* (London: Random House).

Maslow, Abraham (1954). *Motivation and Personality* (New York: Harper).

Miller, George (1956). "The Magical Number Seven, Plus or Minus Two: Some Limits on Our Capacity for Processing Information", *Psychological Review* 63: 81–97.

Minsky, Marvin (1987). *The Society of Mind* (New York: Simon and Schuster).

MIT Center for Collective Intelligence, *Handbook of Collective Intelligence* (available at http://cci.mit.edu/research/handbook.html).

Palmer, Sue (2006). *Toxic Childhood: How the Modern World Is Damaging Our Children and What We Can Do About It* (London: Orion Books).

Perkins, David (1996). *Smart Schools: Better Thinking and Learning for Every Child* (New York: Simon and Schuster).

Peterson, Christopher and Seligman, Martin (2004). *Character Strengths and Virtues: A Handbook and Classification* (New York: American Psychological Association/Oxford University Press).

Pilch, Tony (ed.) (2006). *Neighbourliness* (London: Smith Institute).

Pinker, Stephen (2008). *The Stuff of Thought; Language as a Window into Human Nature* (London: Penguin).

Polanyi, Michael (1958). *Personal Knowledge: Towards a Post-Critical Philosophy* (Chicago: University of Chicago Press).

Putnam, Robert (2000). *Bowling Alone: The Collapse and Revival of American Community* (New York: Simon and Schuster).

Restak, Richard (2004). *The New Brain; How the Modern Age is Rewiring Your Brain* (London: Rodale Ltd).

Revans, Reg (1983). *ABC of Action Learning* (Bromley, Kent: Chartwell-Bratt).

Robinson, Ken and Aronica, Lou (2009). *The Element: How Finding Your Passion Changes Everything* (New York: Penguin).

Rogers, Carl (1969). *Freedom to Learn: A View of What Education Might Become* (1st ed.) (Columbus, OH: Charles Merill).

Rogers, Everett M. (1964). *Diffusion of Innovations* (Glencoe, IL: Free Press).

Rogoff, Barbara (2003). *The Cultural Nature of Human Development* (New York: Oxford University Press USA).

Rotter, Julian (1954). *Social Learning and Clinical Psychology* (New Jersey: Prentice-Hall).

Russell, Bertrand (1928). "On the Value of Scepticism", reprinted in *The Collected Papers of Bertrand Russell*, Vol. 10, ed. John Slater (London: Routledge, 1996).

Sadler-Smith, Eugene (2008). *Inside Intuition* (Oxford: Routledge).

Salomon, Gavriel and Perkins, David (1989). "Rocky Roads to transfer: rethinking mechanisms of a neglected phenomenon", *Educational Psychologist* 24(2): 113–142

Schön, Donald (1983). *Reflective Practitioner: how professionals think in action* (Farnham: Ashgate).

Seligman, Martin (2002). *Learned Optimism: How to Change Your Mind and Your Life* (New York: Simon and Schuster).

Senge, Peter (1990). *The Fifth Discipline: The art and practice of the learning organization* (New York: Doubleday).

Sternberg, Robert (1996). *Successful Intelligence; How Practical and Creative Intelligence Determine Success in Life* (New York: Simon and Schuster).

Toffler, Alvin (1970). *Future Shock* (London: The Bodley Head Ltd).

Whyte, William H. (1952). "Groupthink", *Fortune* magazine, March 1952.

Index

Abilene Paradox 176
accommodation 117
action learning 163–164
Adams, Douglas 14
adaptation 117, 120, 129
adaptive expertise 119
adaptive intelligence 2, 3–4,
        109, 116–143, 153, 221
adaptive self-deception 13
alchemists, modern-day
        150–151
Angelou, Maya 64
Apollo 13 128–129, 136
Appreciative Inquiry 111–113
Argyris, Chris 130, 162
Arnstein, Sherry 208
assimilation 117
Atkinson, Sir William 150
attention deficit disorder 72
Axelrod, Robert 197

Bacon, Francis 157
Bandura, Albert 42, 109–110,
        149–150
Bateson, Gregory 198
Bauch, Andy 118
Bayliss, Trevor 150
Bennis, Warren 198
Binet, Alfred 102
Blackmore, Sarah 12, 13
blogging 87
Bohm, David 210
boiling frog story 32
brainstorming 210
Bransford, John 123

Bronson, Po 171
Bridges, William 49, 53, 58
Bruner, Jerome 208
Buddhism 57

Campaign for Learning 121
Centre for Real-World
        Learning 199
Chabris, Christopher 118
change, four kinds of 6
change, openness to 53
Chinese philosophers 8
choosing 34
Clark, Andy 126
Claxton, Guy 70, 71, 85, 198
Clinton, Bill 37
cognitive dissonance 160–161
Collins, William 73
Columbus, Christopher 13
communities of practice 141–
        142, 221
conscious learning 75
Cooperrider, David 111
congruence 162
Copernicus, Nicholas 13
Costa, Art 28
courage 158
Covey, Stephen 62, 82
creativity 77
Crick, Doug 161
Crosnoe, Robert 52
Csikszentmihalyi, Mihalyi
        76, 77
cyborgs 126

Darwin, Charles 2, 3, 4, 11, 13, 17, 27, 116, 125, 151, 221, 222, 223
Dawkins, Richard 12, 18, 149
de Bono, Edward 136
Dennett, Daniel 127
deferring 82, 84
Deming, W Edwards 105–106, 130
Dewey, John 131
double loop learning 130
Dweck, Carol 16, 101, 104, 156, 171

Edge Foundation 179–180, 188
Einstein, Albert 82, 138
Elder, Glen 53
emotional bank account 63–64
emotional contagion 88
emotions 57
empathy 203–206
Empedocles 8
English language 68
English Project, The 127
Enlightenment, the 48
enquiry (*see also* Inquiry) 111–113, 131
Ericsson, Anders 74
espoused theory 162
ethical mind 195
experimenting 132
expertise, acquisition of 73–74, 75
explanatory style 147
evolutionary engineering 17

facilitation 208–215
family meals, value of 168

feelings of enforced change 51
Festinger, Leon 160
fight or flight 50, 73
flow, state of 76–77
Freire, Paulo 210
Friedman, Thomas 193
Frost, Robert 22

Galton, Francis 151
Gardner, Howard 37, 124, 178, 194, 195
Garratt, Bob 130
Generations X and Y 70, 72, 74
Getty, Jen-Paul 156–157
Gick, Mary 120
Gladwell, Malcolm 45, 94, 149, 151
Gleicher, David 171–173
Gleicher's formula 171–173, 219
goal-setting 154–155
gorilla experiment 118
Greider, William 212
groupthink 174–177
growth mindset 99–100

habit change 24
habits of mind 3, 28, 29, 46, 53, 64, 69, 77, 90, 97, 102, 109, 110, 114, 116, 132, 139, 151, 158, 164, 129, 170, 180, 189, 200, 215, 218, 219
Hallowell, Edward 72
Handy, Charles 150
Harvey, Jerry 176
Hatano, Giyoo 119
Hawken, Paul 207

Heraclitus 8
high road transfer 121
Honey, Peter (*see* learning
     styles) 139–140
Holt, John 123
Hoffer, Eric 27
Holyoak, Keith 120
Honoré, Carl 79
Hopkins, Rob 215
Howell, W. C. 75
humours 9
Hutchins, Robert 200

Illich, Ivan 210
imagining 29
Inagaki, Kayoko 119
inattentional blindness 118
imitation 132
innovation curve 93
intuition 88, 183–184
IQ 39, 48, 101, 102, 124
Irvin, Janis 174

James, William 124
Johnson, Mark 194
Jung, Carl 10

Kallick, Bena 28
Keynes, John Maynard 68
Klein, Gary 183
Kolb, David 138
Kuhn, Thomas 14

ladder of participation 209
Lakoff, George 194
Langer, Ellen 80, 157
Larson, Garry 80
lateral thinking 136

Latham, Gary 155
Lave, Jean 141–142, 198
Law, Andy 151
Law of the Few 152
Leadbeater, Charles 152, 187
learnable intelligence 100
learning organisation 130, 132,
     198
learning styles 139–140
learning transfer 120–123
letting go 53
Lewin, Kurt 16, 49, 50, 58
Lieberman, Mathew 56
locus of control 52, 147
Locke, Edwin 155
low road transfer 121
Luddites 166
Lumet, Sidney 175

Marshmallow test 84, 109
Martin, James 17
Maslow, Abraham 51, 61, 76
meme 12, 101, 149
mere exposure effect 148
Merryman, Ashley 171
Middleton, Julia 151
Milgram, Stanley 176–177
Miller, George 34, 35
mindfulness 157
Mind Gym, The 25
Minsky, Marvin 119
mirror neurons 132, 204
Mischel, Walter 84
Mondale, Walter 104
Montessori, Maria 210
Moore's Law 21, 30
multitasking 74
Mumford, Alan 139–140

Myers, David 88, 167, 180
Myers-Briggs Type Indicator
    10

National College of School
    Leadership 198
needs, hierarchy of 76
neuroscience 132
Nostradamus 11
noticing 31, 54

Obama, Barack 96
On the Origin of the Species 2
Open Space 213–215
Opening Minds curriculum
    123
open-mindedness 156–157
Osborn, Alex 210
Owen, Harrison 213–215

Palmer, Sue 169–170
paradigm shift 14
Parkinson's Law 69
patterns of action 29, 53, 77,
    78, 102, 132,
pause button 82–83
PDSA cycle 105–107
Perkins, David 42, 100, 121
Peters, Tom 96
Peterson, Christopher 158
Piaget, Jean 117
Pinker, Stephen 27, 127, 128
pitching in 200–201
plasticity of the brain 119
Playfulness 80–81
Plus, Minus, Interesting 136
Polanyi, Michael 63

Poldrack, Russell 74
pond weed story 30
positive self-talk 43
praise, overuse of 171
Prisoner's Dilemma game
    196–7
problem-solving 136
Prozac 127
Putnam, Robert 40

Ratey, John 72
Reagan, Ronald 104
rebalancing lives 80
reciprocity principle 196
Rees, Professor Martin 1
reflecting 86, 131
reframing 102
rehearsal 57
relationship capital 62
resilience 59, 60, 158–159
resourcefulness 132
Revans, Reg 163–164
Ritalin 126–127
Rizzolatti, Giaccamo 204
Robinson, Ken 222
Romanticism 48
Rogers, Carl 161–162, 210
Rogers, Everett 92–94, 167
Rogers, Will 149
Rogoff, Barbara 200–201
Rotter, Julian 52, 147
Rowling, J. K. 147
Royal Society of Arts 123,
    188–189
Russell, Bertrand 185

Salomon, Gavriel 121
Sapir–Whorf Hypothesis, 205

Schön, Donald 131
scenario planning 186–187
scepticism 184–185
Seligman, Martin 15, 97–99,
        102, 147, 158
self-discipline 109
The Selfish Gene 12
Senge, Peter 130
Seven Ages of Man 7
Shakespeare, William 6, 7
Shaw, George Bernard 166
Simons, Daniel 118
six degrees of separation 193
Six Thinking Hats 136
Slow Movement 79
SMART goals 155–156
Smith Institute 203
social capital 40, 41
social contagion 132
social intelligence 194
socialising with intent 40
soft focus 86
spiritual dimension 90
Steinbeck, John 162
Sternberg, Robert 124, 125, 153
Stevenson, Robert Louis 170
successful intelligence 124
surfacing 84
synthesising 37

Talent Foundation 188
Tao 8

Tewson, Jane 151
text messaging 87
theory of change 44
theory in use 162
Thorndike, Edward 194
tipping point 94
Tishman, Shari 42
Toffler, Alvin 20, 25, 39
Transition Towns 215
transitions 54, 57
Trivers, Robert 13

unconscious learning 75
unlearning 38

visible thinking 42
Vygotsky, Lev 135, 154

Wagner, Richard 153
Weiss, Carol 44
Wenger, Etienne 141–142, 198
wheel of life 56
Whyte, William 174
woman at the window 23
World Café 210

yin 8, 9
yang 8, 9

Zajonc, Robert 148
zone of proximal development
        135, 154